Start Your Own

PERSONAL CONCIERGE SERVICE

Additional titles in *Entrepreneur's* Startup Series

Start Your Own

Arts and Crafts Business

Automobile Detailing Business

Bar and Club

Bed and Breakfast

Blogging Business

Business of eBay

Business Support Service

Car Wash

Child-Care Service

Cleaning Service

Clothing Store and More

Coaching Business

Coin-Operated Laundry

Construction and Contracting Business

Consulting Business

Crafts Business

Day Spa and More

e-Business

e-Learning Business

Event Planning Business

Executive Recruiting Business

Fashion Accessories Business

Florist Shop and Other Floral Businesses

Food Truck Business

Freelance Writing Business and More

Freight Brokerage Business

Gift Basket Service

Grant-Writing Business

Graphic Design Business

Green Business

Growing and Selling Herbs and Herbal
  Products

Hair Salon and Day Spa

Home Inspection Service

Import/Export Business

Information Consultant Business

Information Marketing Business

Kid-Focused Business

Mail Order Business

Medical Claims Billing Service

Net Services Business

Online Education Business

Personal Concierge Service

Personal Training Business

Pet Business and More

Pet-Sitting Business and More

Photography Business

Public Relations Business

Restaurant and More

Retail Business and More

Self-Publishing Business

Seminar Production Business

Senior Services Business

Specialty Travel and Tour Business

Staffing Service

Tutoring and Test Prep Business

Vending Business

Wedding Consultant Business

Wholesale Distribution Business

Entrepreneur
MAGAZINE'S

startup

Start Your Own

3RD EDITION

PERSONAL CONCIERGE SERVICE

Your Step-by-Step Guide to Success

Entrepreneur Press and Ciree Linsenman

Ep
Entrepreneur Press

Jere L. Calmes, Publisher
Cover Design: Beth Hansen-Winter
Production and Composition: Eliot House Productions

This publication is designed to provide accurate and authoritative information in regard to the subject matter covered. It is sold with the understanding that the publisher is not engaged in rendering legal, accounting or other professional services. If legal advice or other expert assistance is required, the services of a competent professional person should be sought.

Library of Congress Cataloging-in-Publication Data
Linsenman, Ciree.
Start your own personal concierge service/by Entrepreneur Press and Ciree Linsenman.—3rd ed.
p. cm.
Rev. ed. of: Start your own personal concierge service : your step-by-step guide to success/ Entrepreneur Press and Heather Heath Dismore.
Includes index.
ISBN-13: 978-1-59918-425-8 (alk. paper)
ISBN-10: 1-59918-425-7 (alk. paper)
1. Personal concierges. 2. Small business—Management. I. Dismore, H. (Heather). Start your own personal concierge service. II. Entrepreneur Press. III. Title.
HD9999.P3942A33 2011
640—dc23   2011021184

Printed in the United States of America

15 14 13 12 11   10 9 8 7 6 5 4 3 2 1

Contents

Appendix

Preface

You're the type of person who can juggle ten different projects at once and make sure they all turn out well. Everything you touch shines a little brighter when you're done. You make friends wherever you go. You thrive on deadlines and love a challenge. But after years of racing around the corporate fast track, you're ready to pursue new challenges and set your own course. And you think a personal concierge service might be your track to independence and success.

A personal concierge service runs on the most basic of premises. People want things done but don't have time to do them.

But they are happy to pay someone to take care of their business efficiently and with a touch of class. Why not let that someone be you?

You are probably reading this book after thinking long and hard about starting your own business. You are excited, anxious, maybe even scared—all natural emotions when considering such a lifestyle change. Although we can't make the big leap for you, we can give you the information to help you plan your next step.

Our mission is to provide all the facts you need to:

- Decide if a personal concierge service is the right business for you.
- Promote your business for maximum results.
- Start your new business on the right foot.
- Keep your business on the track to success.

You've probably wondered what it's really like to be a personal concierge. Wouldn't it be great to actually talk to one and find out what a day in his or her life is like? What's the best part of the job? What's the most challenging? The most fun? Well, in this book you will hear from personal concierges who share their stories, tips, and a few secrets. You'll even hear some of the more unusual requests personal concierges have received. (Sorry, you'll have to wait for those tantalizing details until further along in the book.)

This business guide also includes worksheets to help you estimate startup expenses and operating costs, ideas about organizing your business, tips on how to find and keep clients, and even a feature called Stat Fact, which highlights interesting statistics about the personal concierge industry.

We hope that you are ready to learn everything about the world of personal concierges and that you are enthusiastic about venturing into a business where you can carve out your own niche. Your new career will be exactly what you make it. And there's no reason why you can't be the next in-demand personal concierge. But first, you've got some reading to do. So jump right in. This is going to be fun!

Keeper of
the Candles
Industry Overview

In this chapter, we'll explore the new trend toward personal concierge services as well as the history of the concierge profession as a whole. We'll also introduce you to several entrepreneurs who have started their own personal concierge services. You'll benefit from their experience and advice as we look into the personal concierge industry.

Spreading Like Wildfire

Concierges have been around in one form or another for centuries, but the personal concierge burst onto the scene only in the late 1990s. Today, more people have less time for everyday tasks, and many of them rely on personal concierges for everything from walking the dog to getting dinner on the table. There are few tasks a personal concierge won't tackle, as long as the chore is legal, of course.

Although personal concierge services are a fairly recent development, the number of companies that serve time-starved clients is mushrooming, right along with customer demand for such businesses. Today's stressed

> **Fun Fact**
>
> Pronouncing the word concierge may seem intimidating. OK, on three: one, two, three—kon'se erzh. If you want a good laugh, just ask a concierge how many variations of the pronunciation he or she has heard.

workers, trying to catch up financially, are working longer hours and it just makes sense to hire help. Membership in the National Association of Professional Organizers, which includes some professionals who provide concierge services, swelled from a few hundred when founded in 1985 to more than 4,000 members to date.

The International Concierge and Lifestyle Management Association (ICLMA), an association of 350 lifestyle management professionals, found some optimistic results in their 2010 annual global concierge survey. Of the 207 respondents, the U.S. respondents reported that 37.5 percent of their business was comprised of errands and personal shopping requests, with general home management coming in at a close second at 35 percent.

Why the booming demand for personal concierges and organizers? A big reason is that most people are incredibly busy with jobs, families, and/or maintaining a household. Some people need help just to get organized; others could manage the paperwork if they were not saddled with so many other chores, and still others would love to have the time and freedom to achieve lofty personal goals, which they use niche concierges for. That is when they turn to (or would like to be able to turn to) professionals to help keep them organized, run errands, and see to it that business and personal obligations are met. They will look to personal concierges to help relieve stress and bring order to hectic lives.

Katharine Giovanni, Chairman of the Board and founder of the ICLMA, and award winning concierge author of *The Concierge Manual: A Step-by-Step Guide to Starting Your Own Concierge Service or Lifestyle Management Company* (New Road Publishing, 2007), has this to say about the future of the concierge industry: "Despite the current economy, the independent concierge industry is growing . . . and it's growing at a steady pace around the world, though not in every country, through all major markets.

Companies are offering this unique service as a part of their corporate benefit package and as an additional service for their clients. Globally, real estate management companies offer an active concierge on site in the lobbies of their buildings so they can outshine their competition. The industry is also growing like a brush fire in hospitals around the United States, though not as fast outside the U.S. Security guards are being cross-trained to double as concierges. Shopping malls are offering concierge desks and kiosks. Fortune 500 companies like American Express, Google, and Coldwater Creek are all offering concierge services to staff and/or customers. There are hundreds more. This service is popping up everywhere, from funeral homes, train stations, and shopping malls, to hospitals, hospice care facilities, and even in nonprofits."

As our industry expands we are seeing franchises, too, such as My Girl Friday (www.egirlfriday.com) and Quintessentially (www.quintessentially.com), which is also currently the industry's largest international concierge company. The internet concierge trend is also developing rapidly, a prime example of which is WOW! Branded Personal Assistance (www.thewowcard.com).

Although it's no secret that the personal concierge field is booming, hard numbers are difficult to come by. The National Concierge Association, founded in Chicago in the late 1990s as a networking and resource organization for both personal and hotel concierges, doesn't yet track numbers or statistics pertaining to the industry, but membership has grown from six members in 1998 to over 600.

Katharine Giovanni quantifies the industry, "You can actually see the phenomenal growth by looking at my company's numbers. Triangle Concierge began in 1998 with a dozen clients. Today we have thousands of clients from 40 countries and every U.S. state." Several other personal concierges and concierge consultants agreed with that estimate and said the number of personal concierges is growing fast.

According to Sara-ann Kasner, founder and CEO of the National Concierge Association (www.nationalconciergeassociation.com), "The concierge business is exploding right now. There has been tremendous growth." Personal concierges and industry analysts say there is plenty of room for even more growth.

Shifting Gears

Many successful concierges do not have a hotel background. In fact those interviewed for this book came from such disparate backgrounds as customer service, events management, legal assistants, law enforcement officers, executive recruiting, and executive assistants. Jennifer Knoch of Radar Virtual Concierge (www.radar-msp.com) in Minneapolis, Minnesota, has an innate set of concierge skills: creative thinking, a sense of urgency, attention to detail, and follow-through. She first used those skills in customer service, project management, and production and now finds that they serve her well in catering to clients' needs. Jennifer specializes in holiday gift buying assistance and it takes an artistic eye combined with the right communication skills to deliver consistently to her time-challenged gift givers.

Valerie Fidan's background as a personal assistant for male Fortune 500 executives, lawyers, entrepreneurs, and sports figures prepared her for success in her male-specific luxury concierge service, Valerie A. Lifestyle Management (www.valeriea.com).

Kevin Miller of The Daily Plan It, Inc. (www.thedailyplanit.info) says his background as an American Express office assistant and computer research gopher, combined with ownership of a small grocery store, developed the skills he now uses with the gay, senior demographic he caters to in Fort Lauderdale, Florida.

As a practitioner in the alternative health sector, Brian Mahan's skills came in handy developing the eco-conscious, health-oriented Enlightened Concierge (www.enlightenedconcierge.com) in West Hollywood, California. He put his connections in the health industry and networking skills to use to create a topnotch team of alternative health professionals for his clients to access, all in one place.

Silvia Oppenheim's San Francisco, California, full service, hospitality company, Le Concierge SF (www.leconciergesf.com), features everything from event catering and professional organizing to relocation services. Her background managing high

Crafty Characters Excel

A wonderful historical example of how the character and skills of a concierge were developed in one Madame Lucie at the turn of the century is revealed in the fascinating book, *Confessions of a Concierge, Madame Lucie`s History of Twentieth-Century France*, by Bonnie G. Smith (Yale University Press, 1987). This work shows how the limitations of growing up in wartime stoked the deep roots of creativity to blossom for what would make Madame Lucie a genius, an unflappable concierge of almost magician status. One of the many illustrations of creativity born from necessity in the book paints the picture of Lucie and her father catching their dinner of eels by lowering an umbrella baited with a hand-sewn "worm ball" in a river, waiting for just the right moment to slap shut the device, trapping dinner for the family.

While your own life may not contain such dramatic examples, you may ask yourself how many times you've used creativity to change the situation you're in. The ability to change nothing into something, and use whatever you have to make the seemingly impossible happen, is one of the most vital skills a concierge has.

profile accounts at the Ritz-Carlton and private estates for Fortune 500 clients and commodity trading in a cutthroat business environment primed her with the chutzpah she'd later use to excel in completing the most challenging client requests.

Ancient Roots

Although more and more people are becoming familiar with the term "concierge," very few know where this customer service-based profession originated. The word "concierge" evolved from the French *comte des cierges*, the "keeper of the candles," a term that referred to the servant who attended to the whims of visiting noblemen at medieval castles. Eventually, the name "concierge" came to stand for the keepers of the keys at public buildings, especially hotels. There is even a famous prison in Paris that is called The Conciergerie, in honor of the warden who kept the keys and assigned cells to the inmates.

The stigma of the concierge has changed greatly since the early 1900s where service personnel known as concierges first showed up in small rental apartments, then in some luxury hotels in Europe. Then, as now, their duties were to welcome and assist guests throughout their stay. In the small residential rentals a concierge would facilitate everything possible to help the building's residents, from laundry services to obtaining their most unusual purchases. In Madame Lucie's case, before she actually became a concierge herself, she was tutored by watching a neighborhood concierge who seemed to know everything about everyone on their street and used the information to get things to happen. Sound familiar?

Today's professionals may not operate to that end but the importance of keeping social connections strong can't be stressed enough when trying to build solid vendor connections in this world of "You scratch my back, I'll scratch yours." Naturally, guests didn't have as many options or services as they do today. Traditionally, male concierges were mostly found in

> **Tip...**
>
> **Smart Tip**
>
> Reports from the field: In a 2009 *New York Times* interview, the top residential concierges in The Big Apple commented that even though client service requests have changed to reflect economic hardship, the phone still keeps ringing, but with different kinds of requests. Request for economical services include finding reliable shoe repair (when previously clients would have just purchased new ones), restructuring already existing clothing to feel like a new wardrobe (clients in the past would have purchased more new wardrobe pieces), nixing the lavish dinner parties and requesting private party room rental at affordable local restaurants or cutting their guest lists back from 100 to more an intimate 20.

the better hotels. Today, a 70 percent female to 30 percent male concierge ratio operates in the United States, while in Europe the concierge industry remains predominantly male.

Defining Moment

To fully understand the industry, it's important to make the distinction between hotel concierges, corporate concierges, and personal concierges (we'll be focusing on the latter in this book).

Hotel concierges are employed by hotels to assist guests by arranging tours, making dinner reservations, offering advice on shopping or sightseeing, and taking care of other needs that may arise during their stay. At this time, only hotel concierges may become members of the elite Les Clefs d'Or (pronounced "lay clay door"), a professional organization of hotel concierges all over the world. To join, applicants must have at least five years of hotel lobby-level employment, with at least three of those years as a concierge. Applicants must also pass a written test, submit letters of recommendation, and pass test calls by examiners who pose as hotel guests.

Of the approximately 5,000 hotel concierges in the United States, 160 applied to join Les Clefs d'Or in a recent year, and only 25 were accepted. Les Clefs d'Or means "the keys of gold," and it's the emblem adopted by the association of concierges founded in Paris in 1929. Hence the gold keys pins that you will see on the lapels of

> **Fun Fact**
>
> The U.S. branch of the Les Clefs d'Or have hosted, sponsored, and led symposia and full semester-long courses at many of the most prestigious hospitality programs in the country, including Cornell University, University of Nevada-Las Vegas, Penn State, and Johnson & Wales.

concierges who are members of Les Clefs d'Or. If a hotel concierge is ever found guilty of an ethical breach, such as accepting commissions from restaurants or other companies, he or she is banned from the group for life and must surrender the gold keys.

Corporate concierges are employed by a corporation to serve the firm's employees. The niche for corporate concierges grew out of the desire of some corporations to keep their employees so happy that they would never leave for greener pastures. In the quest for worker satisfaction, some companies have hired concierges to help employees with planning business trips, picking up dry cleaning, ordering dinner, running errands, and so on. Dentists, psychologists, massage therapists, and others are even offering their services in the workplace through concierges.

A personal concierge is not employed by a hotel or corporation. Instead, these men and women market their services directly to clients who pay them for running errands, buying gifts, making travel arrangements, or myriad other tasks. Some of their clients may, however, be corporations, which contract with them to be available for employee requests.

While personal concierges typically appeal to a different market than those in hotels or corporations, their markets sometimes overlap. For instance, a businessperson may use the services of a hotel concierge while traveling and the services of a personal concierge after returning home.

Typically, a personal concierge builds a client base that uses his or her services on a regular basis. Clients might mostly be individual consumers, or predominately small businesses. They could even be a combination of the two. The personal concierge business is so new and evolving so quickly that no hard and fast rules exist. Again, this business is definitely what you make it. (You'll read more about defining the personal concierge market in Chapter 2.)

Striking While the Iron Is Hot

No official numbers are available on just how many people work as general, personal concierges. Below are some stats on similar professions as reported in 2008 by the Bureau of Labor Statistics (BLS). While considering how much you might make as a personal, general, or specialty concierge, take a look at the sampling of rates we've also gathered from thriving concierges today. Add to that, the knowledge that anytime you reach the level in your career where you are actually managing instead of just assisting, your income has the potential to skyrocket. "Lifestyle management" is a term used to define a concierge who literally manages your life. To be that, you must hone your service model to be all-inclusive, addictive, and indispensable. These facts point to promising opportunities for industrious, creative types interested in creating a fulfilling career in this industry.

- More and more hotel concierges, after learning every aspect of the trade, are walking away from their jobs to start their own personal concierge businesses.
- The internet has made it easier for entrepreneurs to succeed in far-flung fields. For example, the internet allows a personal concierge in Idaho to target potential clients in Louisiana—or even Paris.
- Many concierge networks and associations exist today, when just one was around 13 years ago.
- 2009 national median salaries for hotel, apartment, and office concierges as reported by the Bureau of Labor Statistics were $13 an hour and projected growth by 2018 is higher than average.

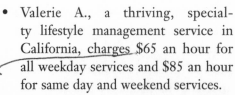

- Valerie A., a thriving, specialty lifestyle management service in California, charges $65 an hour for all weekday services and $85 an hour for same day and weekend services.

- The Montana Concierge, a service catering to vacationers, business visitors, residents, and local businesses, charges $25 to $60 an hour for a combination of professional business, event, and domestic assistance services.

- Travel guides, who require many of the same skills as lifestyle management professionals and hotel concierges, were reported to have national median pay rates of $15 an hour, or $31,000 annually, according to a Bureau of Labor Statistics 2009 report.

- Though the BLS also reports personal home care aides as taking in an average of $9.46 an hour in 2009, the growth for this field is projected as much higher than average. Catering to this crowd by offering similar services in addition to all of the other one-stop-shop perks you're probably thinking of offering right now could position you to be attractive to those who have need, but also the income to pay a much higher rate for a "lifestyle management" professional than a personal care attendant doing many of the same duties.

- Silvia Oppenheim of Le Concierge SF works a 40-hour work-week, charges $50 to $75 an hour, and reports an annual salary in the neighborhood of $100,000.

Tip...

Smart Tip

Combining the offerings of a few specialty fields, like "personal shopper" and "personal assistant" can create just the right tailored concierge service to offer your specific demographic. Payscale.com utilizes nationally donated salary information from many fields and locations. If you'd like to imagine what services would pay well in a certain area or how to combine several services to compete with local thrivers, play a little on www.payscale.com. Punch in your desired location and choose several free occupational salary reports. Defining your concierge profile should be based on client needs, how much money your customers have, and how much money you want to make. They need to match up!

Personal concierges who live in small towns or who reach out to clients outside their immediate geographic area generally have contacts and resources near those locations to handle the hands-on work. Concierge businesses can offer a smorgasbord of services or specialize in one or two areas. For instance, some personal concierges organize clients' cluttered desks, set up their offices, and help them manage their schedules. Others offer to do everything from standing in line at the Department of Motor Vehicles to helping set up an elaborate marriage proposal. Some concierge businesses specialize in wedding planning, shopping for and wrapping gifts, and decorating for the holidays. Some offer pet-sitting services. Other specialize in elder-care services, like accompanying seniors to doctors appointments, picking up prescriptions, or driving them to hair appointments. The list of services is endless, and it changes every day.

One reason more people are using the services of personal concierges is that their free time is fading away faster than ever. As a rule, most of us have less personal time than in years past. How many times have you heard the refrain "There just aren't enough hours in the day"? Hence, the demand for helpers to run errands for us just becomes more desperate. More than ever, families include two full-time wage earners, and even many teenagers hold down part-time jobs. Who will get dinner on the table, pick up the dry cleaning, get the dog groomed, and make sure the lawn gets mowed on a regular basis if everyone is at work? Can you say "concierge?"

According to the concierges interviewed for this book, people who make the best concierges share certain characteristics: They're patient, calm, resourceful, have good contacts, and enjoy people. If that sounds like you, and you like having a different routine every day, juggling multiple projects, and making people happy, this could be the business for you. We'll talk a lot more about what it takes to be a concierge and explore a typical day in the life of a concierge in Chapter 6.

Some personal concierges say the field was so new when they started their businesses that there were few experts to turn to for advice. The few people already established in

Concierge Conundrum

A client orders a special piece of jewelry and asks his personal concierge to pick up the piece so he can present it to his wife at a dinner party that evening. The concierge gets to the store and finds it closed for inventory. Panic? Not a concierge. He pulls out his Rolodex and gets busy. It takes two hours, but he eventually locates the owner of the store who agrees to open it so the concierge can retrieve the jewelry. The client? None the wiser, he gets his piece of jewelry on time. The wife? Happy as a clam. The concierge? Ends up with a fat tip.

the field were often reluctant to give away any secrets for fear of competition. As the field grew, more resources became available to anyone looking for ideas about setting up a personal concierge business; you can find some of these listed in the Appendix of this book.

You Need That When?

A personal concierge's duties can be as simple as gift-shopping for a client or as elaborate as arranging to have a Rolls Royce waiting at the airport to whisk a client and his girlfriend to a hotel room stocked with six dozen red roses, chilled champagne, a catered prime rib dinner, and a camera to record her reaction when he proposes.

Personal concierges are people with connections. They know how to get front-row tickets to a concert that has been sold out for weeks. They know whom to call when a client isn't happy with the color of his rental car and wants a fire engine red convertible delivered now. They don't panic when a client calls with a last-minute request for a private jet. They have Rolodexes that read like a who's who. Most important, they perform well under pressure and almost always get the job done—politely and with a smile.

Personal concierges aren't just for people with deep pockets. Time-saving perks are enjoyed by all sorts. In a sense, people who employ a personal concierge are buying back their own time, and who can't benefit from that? A personal concierge's clients might include everyone from corporate millionaires and hotshot celebrities to couples with two incomes but zero free time to single moms holding down two jobs. One client may require the services of a personal concierge only a couple of hours a month, while another client may insist that the concierge be available at all times.

Well, Isn't That Convenient?

According to the concierges interviewed for this book, most people don't have a clear picture of what a concierge is. Many people understand the concept once you explain it to them, and think it's a great business idea. Jennifer C. of Gainesville, Georgia, says she was "shocked that [potential clients] didn't pick up on it as expected. I spend a lot of time educating them about what we do, teaching people about my business. You have to break them of the habit of doing the errands themselves. Once they get used to you, they can't live without you."

Kathy S. in Elkhart, Indiana, knows it's important to anticipate clients' needs before they even voice them. She tells of one client who works from home, but travels extensively. "I take care of her cat quite a bit. Once she was out of town and I noticed she was running low on her favorite tea. I made sure she was restocked before she returned home."

Reaping the Rewards

Almost every concierge we talked to loved their job and is so glad they took the plunge. One concierge worked with lawyers in her previous profession and found that they were always critical. In her current business, everything she does makes her clients happy. "I love knowing that what I'm doing means something to people." Another notes the variety as key to her job satisfaction, "I face a new challenge every day, and it keeps my brain fresh. Also, there is a great privilege associated with earning a client's trust enough that they allow you access to their most personal affairs."

Even though being a personal concierge is, by all accounts, a rewarding job, it can also be a stressful one. "The hardest thing about the job is keeping all the details straight," says Cynthia A., the concierge in San Diego. "You have a lot of balls in the air; the more successful you are, the more balls you have in the air."

Stat Fact

According to a recent study by the Families and Work Institute, 44 percent of workers are overworked some of the time or most of the time. What does this mean for personal concierges? The less free time clients have, the more likely they are to rely on concierge services.

Think of a concierge as someone who can attend to the little—and the big—details of life for people who don't have the time to attend to the details themselves.

Bringing Home the Dough

Personal concierges can expect to make anywhere from $10,000 to $125,000 a year, conservatively. (Once they've built a clientele, $40,000 to $60,000 each year is more realistic for those working full time). However, businesses with annual incomes of $125,000 or more are not unheard of, depending on their location, the clients they take on, and the range of services they offer. In addition, concierges often receive tips or gifts from grateful clients.

Concierges bill their clients in a variety of ways. For instance, some charge membership fees based on how many requests are usually made per month. Others bill on monthly retainers, while others charge per service or per hour. Most we spoke to billed by the hour. It's your game, and you can tailor it to meet your needs.

When asked to put numbers to their fees, concierges say their typical charges work out to be anywhere from $20 to $125 an hour, depending on the particular task and the geographic location of their business. For example, rates are typically higher in urban areas than in rural areas. If concierges dip into their own money to purchase something for a client, the client is billed for the item later.

Some personal concierges also receive what are known as referral fees from various companies when they steer business to them. Companies that often pay referral fees include wedding planners, caterers, and florists. Many concierges will pick up extra income via this avenue.

Start Me Up

By now, you must be wondering what kind of hard cash it takes to get started in the personal concierge business. As with many businesses, it all depends on how you decide to get started. Depending on whether or not you take advantage of the many free services and tricks available to save money, and how you communicate with your clients, startup costs for a personal concierge business are estimated to be between virtually free and $5,000. If you already own all of your communication hardware and software, like a computer and cell phone and possibly a printer and fax, you've got a head start. If you also plan on keeping much of your communication, advertising, billing, and social marketing on the virtual front, then you don't even need a printer or fax, but we'll get to some of those money-saving tricks later in the book. If not, the figure could be considerably higher, depending on what kind of computer system and other office supplies you choose to buy.

Since it is a service-based business rather than a product-based one that calls for inventory, starting a personal concierge business doesn't require a large financial investment. In fact, much of what you'll need to be a good concierge can't be bought—for instance, the contacts that come from long-term business relationships with the right people. You can't put a price tag on those contacts, but having them puts you well on the way to success.

You'll still need all the basics, though. In addition to a computer, items such as office supplies, reference materials, postage, stationery, business cards, phone, voice mail, and internet access are vital. We'll have a lot more on equipping your office in Chapter 5.

Ready for the next step? In Chapter 2, we take a look at just how hot the personal concierge market is and why those fabulous assistants are popping up just about everywhere, including the corporate world.

> ### Fun Fact
> Did you know that concierges often rub elbows with celebrities? Shhh, don't tell anyone. Concierges never do. Well, they're not supposed to, anyway. For some reason, though, Michael Fazio gets away with dishing behind-the-scenes gossip as an assistant to the rich and famous in his book, *Concierge Confidential: The Gloves Come Off—and the Secrets Come Out! Tales from the Man Who Serves Millionaires, Moguls, and Madmen,* (St. Martin's Press, 2011).

2

People Who Need People
Defining Your Market

Who uses personal concierges? Everyone from the millionaire corporate chairperson to the single mom with two jobs and three children under age ten. In a sense, people who employ a personal concierge are buying back their own time, and who can't benefit from that? This chapter shows you the importance of identifying your prospective clients, what their needs are, and the services you will provide for them.

Although the term "concierge" used to be associated mostly with upscale hotels, concierges are now found in many different settings. In this chapter, we'll show you some of the settings where you'll find concierges, and look at some of the hottest trends in the industry. Let's kick start your niche development process. The perfect match for your innate personality traits and experience is out there in many forms. The options are endless!

Perks and More Perks

In today's competitive job market, employers are finding that they not only need to create a safe and supportive environment for their employees, but that they must also give employees benefits that help them balance the demands of work and personal commitments. Some companies have found that their employees are putting in so much overtime, committing to crazy business travel schedules, and working such long hours that they don't have enough hours left in the week to attend to personal business. Employers in certain fields, such as insurance, banking, and manufacturing, have found that offering help to their time-stretched employees can boost productivity, making this a workplace perk that benefits the business as well as the workers.

For this reason, more employers are offering personal concierge services to their employees. If an employee knows he won't have time to cook or stop for dinner on the way home from work, he can pick up the phone and call his company's personal concierge service to order dinner and have it delivered—leaving the work to the concierge. Or if the salesperson is on the road and has to extend her trip another few days, she can pick up the phone and make sure her landscaping needs are taken care of

Smart Tip

Tip...

Most of the concierges we interviewed felt that the fact that we are just coming out of a recession only helps the outlook for the concierge industry. People have had to work harder in the last five years to either keep their jobs, recover from a layoff and get a new job, or sometimes double up on two careers just to make ends meet. The positive, though small, improvements in the economy uplifts spirits and encourage a bit more spending. Hardworking, busy people now generally have slightly more money to spend than just a few years ago, but still appreciate a great deal, still feeling vulnerable to what the last five years has wrought on our lives.

This should give you an idea for a niche. How about being an economic concierge? Your services save your clients some money because you know all the best places to shop for them and your crafty, well-written blog is loaded with ideas to save them time and even more money. You'll read about blogging in Chapter 9.

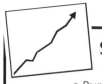

Stat Fact
According to a Bureau of Labor Statistics' 2008 through 2018 report, home health aides and personal and home care aides were the third and fourth most rapidly growing fields. If caring for those recovering from hospital stays, the elderly and mentally or physically challenged calls out to your heart, shaping your concierge business to offer some of the services desired by this needy market would make good business sense.

while she's gone. Industry experts predict we'll be seeing more and more personal concierges serving businesses in the near future. These personal concierges are not to be confused with corporate concierges; they are not actually corporate employees—more like corporate suppliers. Personal concierge operators are contracted by corporations to provide concierge services, either on-site or on call.

Every concierge we spoke with believes that the outlook for the concierge market is bright. Four of the concierges we interviewed advised catering to the huge baby boomer crowd. They see a big demand for services like elder care, senior dating, and relocation help, to mention a few. Silvia Oppenheim of Le Concierge SF, in San Francisco, California, has noticed a growing need for added personal chef services among her clients. Though she provides a host of well-used general services ranging from professional organizing, travel, and event planning to first time parent coaching, the feedback she's seeing from her chef services are standing out. "People are starting to see that for around $375 a week, for a family of three, it's worth it for them to hire me to take care of everything in the kitchen. For that rate they get shopping, menu planning, and complete, healthy meals prepared in their own kitchen (with leftovers to nibble on later!), including dessert. While that doesn't include the cost of the groceries, it's a major time investment, so for people who are time challenged and have health goals, it's a great deal."

Kellye G. sees concierges in the "lobbies of office buildings, offered in employee compensation packages, and in hospitals." It's just one more tool corporations are finding helpful in a competitive job market as they try to woo potential candidates to their companies—and then try to keep employees happy once they're on board.

Stat Fact
Best Upon Request (www.bestuponrequest .com), an award winning onsite corporate concierge service, reports the beneficial findings from a 2007 study of corporate concierge services used by nurses and other health care industry professionals with these figures: Over 93 percent of employees said concierge services helped reduce their stress levels, more than 92 percent said it helped them balance work and personal responsibilities, and 94 percent said that these services increased their commitment to their employers.

Even if you don't have a contract with a corporation, you can still target many corporate employees who need some extra help. For instance, one savvy personal concierge set up shop in a corner of a busy Chicago office building and specialized in filling grocery orders for busy secretaries and executives who never had time to get their food shopping done. She had helpers who bought the nonperishables and returned with them by the end of the day. The enterprising concierge then had other helpers load everything up into her van, which she set up in the employee parking lot as her clients were leaving work. Her clients picked up their groceries; she picked up her checks—and everyone was happy.

One Call Does It All

Another hot trend is the emergence of personal concierges in the real estate world. Some real estate brokerage firms are contracting personal concierge services to provide home buyers with everything from the disconnection of their utilities and dismantling and packing of everything at their old residence to everything they need upon arrival at their new home. Services not only include hooking-up utilities and moving in, but staging, redecorating, cleaning, shopping and establishing connections to all of those homeowner services like pool cleaning, lawn mowing, and pet care that homeowners spend countless hours scouring the internet for, just looking for reliable professionals. The fact that the homebuyer makes a single phone call to get all of this done is pretty seductive and starts the cycle of dependence. What's not to like about that? (Hint: Read about relocation concierges at length in Chapter 3.) Many real estate firms put together a network of local vendors, such as dry cleaners, florists, and bakers, who offer the real estate customers their services at discounted prices. Many are expanding these services to include full relocation assistance such as restaurant and salon recommendations, interior design consulting, nearby childcare providers, and help with locating places of worship. A personal concierge can become the link between the real estate customer and the dozens (or hundreds) of vendors on the brokerage's list, allowing the customer to take care of dozens of errands with just one phone call.

Real estate giant Coldwell Banker has developed its own service, Coldwell Banker Concierge, to help its clients move seamlessly from one home to another. Services range from locksmithing, carpet installations, and maid service to providing feng shui masters. Personal concierges increasingly provide the bridge between customers and the services being offered by real estate firms. You could be the provider for a smaller boutique real estate broker in your area that wants to provide premier service to his clients.

Some experts predict it won't be long before the concierge concept will be in virtually every real estate market in the country. In fact, some real estate companies have already begun referring to themselves as being in the home services business instead of the real estate business.

The trend doesn't stop with residential real estate. As revitalization of downtown areas occurs across the country, more people are choosing downtown living, often in high rise condos and luxury apartments. You could provide services for tenants in those buildings. If you can make inroads with a developer in your area, you could specialize in servicing these locations. You do realize what this means for you, right? Just one more niche you can specialize in! With the field exploding the way it is, you can expect that similar opportunities may crop up down the road.

If you want to start a personal concierge business in the real estate industry, you could offer to provide some of the services we mentioned above. For instance, if you have sources who know a lot about feng shui, you might offer feng shui; if you have some contacts in the locksmith field, think about providing locksmithing services. Again, the possibilities are absolutely endless.

Finding Your Niche

As an aspiring personal concierge, you need to decide what your niche will be. For instance, will you cater strictly to corporate clients? Will you specialize in particular areas for clients or offer more broad-based services? Some personal concierges specialize in one area, such as lining up tickets for concerts or special events; others pride themselves on running every errand imaginable. You need to spend some time thinking about what type of service you want to provide.

After thinking about what you want to do, take it a step further and write out a formal mission statement for your business. The statement should define your goals and lay out your plans for your business. Complete the Mission Statement Worksheet on page 22 and assignments in Chapter 3 for help getting started on your own.

Kellye G., the personal concierge in Ft. Worth, Texas, notes that finding her niche was one of the biggest challenges when she started her business. "It took a solid month and the luck of a perfect referral," she says, to get her on the path to success. On a typical day, she spends 9 A.M. to 1 P.M. with a permanent weekday client, then spends the afternoon working with other clients and building her business through prospecting for clients, writing proposals, and updating her website.

Katharine G. says that her clients are almost exclusively corporate clients and that her company often provides errand services. "We'll pick up people's groceries and prescriptions, go to the post office, do light—and I emphasize light—housekeeping, make phone calls, personal shopping, pick up meals, and run various other errands," Katharine continues, "We also do event planning, weddings, parties, expos, and things of that nature. And we have a business referral service that is very popular. I think personal concierges help to take the stress off of people's shoulders. The need for concierges has arisen from the simple fact that we are all just so busy today."

Valerie Fidan of San Francisco has found a niche for herself with the male movers and shakers group in the Bay Area needing assistance with everything from wardrobe consultation to date planning. She talks about using her skills to serve an all-male client base, "Men are problem solvers and want things done. They want solutions. Women are more proactive at getting things done and are great at multi-tasking. I wouldn't say that men are easier to work with; in fact, sometimes they are more difficult to work with because you have to play the role of a psychic and have mind-reading ability! Sometimes they say one thing but mean the complete opposite! It's just a matter of getting to know the client and really understanding what they really want!"

> **Tip...**
>
> ### Smart Tip
> There is no point in trying to make all your clients fit into one neat little category, especially if you don't intend to specialize in the corporate arena. Your clients may be family members, old friends, the pediatrician who has known you since you were three, and your sixth-grade teacher's next-door neighbor. You get the idea—the possibilities are endless. Keep an open mind and an eye out for new possibilities, and then watch your business soar.

What It Takes

A good dose of business savvy goes a long way in this business. Most concierges we spoke with had challenges with starting a new business, just like anyone would regardless of industry. "The first year of any business is very difficult. You must work really hard and spend a lot of money on advertising that doesn't always pay off initially. You are constantly having to prove yourself to establish the trust that this industry demands," notes one concierge fairly new to the industry.

Silvia Oppenheim advises new concierges to be ready to do anything for your clients to prove you're there for them and can meet any challenges they present. She recalls turning herself inside out to provide a fairly new client with a strange request. Her new client, in the middle of negotiating a $500,000 deal, noted that the man with the checkbook expressed a desire for a Slurpee. He decided to try out his new concierge and found that nothing could stop Silvia, as she delivered the icy cold slush an hour later and impressed the wealthy Texan enough to get him to lend his signature to that $500,000 check. Behind the scenes, it wasn't so smooth. Silvia had hurriedly searched high and low for a 7-11—the only place that carries Slurpees. She wound up calling a friend across town, who purchased the drink, then drove it to another friend, who handed it off to Silvia, just in the nick of time. It pays to know people and to be willing to do anything to fulfill a client request. She now had a client for life.

Get Educated

There are many types of education that will prime you to shine in your field, from simple training videos and on-the-job learning to the more formal certificate programs offered by hospitality institutes and specialty schools. Studying how other specialty concierges set up their businesses will help you figure out which services you want to offer or avoid. Below is a list of suggestions for education relating to the type of concierge work you decide to do.

Concierge Education Suggestions	
Household, High-End Personal Concierge	Starkey International Institute's Private Service Household Management and Personal Assistant Certifications, (www.starkeyintl.com), Platinum Lifestyle Management (www.platinumlm.com), Vivez La Vie, Inc. (www.vivezlavie.com)
General Household Concierge	Legally Organized (www.legallyorganized.com), Rent A Smile (www.rentasmile.com), Concierge Medical Training (www.conciergemedicaltraining.com), Head Concierge (www.headconcierge.com), Belavie (www.mybelavie.com)
Elder Concierge	Check-In Calls (www.checkincalls.com), Senior Concierge (www.seniorconciergeny.com), Golden Concierge LLC (www.goldenconciergellc.com), Caregiver's Home Companion (www.caregivershome.com), Elder Care Online (www.ec-online.net)
Family Child and Pet Concierge	Whole Nine (www.wholeninelifestyle.com), Dream Weaver (www.dreamweaverconcierge.com), Konowitz, Kahn and Company, P.C. (www.konowitzkahn.com), Lifestyle Caddy (www.lifestylecaddy.com), Call On Jack (www.callonjack.com)

Concierge Education Suggestions, continued

Relocation Concierge	Running In Stilettos (www.runninginstilettoslkn.com), Sense and Order (www.senseandorder.com), Concierge Relocation (www.conciergerelocation.com), Wittz End (www.atwittzend.com)
Green Concierge	HR Green (www.hrgreenblog.com), GreenerPenny (www.greenerpenny.com), Responsible Consumer (www.responsibleconsumer.net), Treehugger (www.treehugger.com), Natural Home (www.natural homemagazine.com), Inhabitat (www.inhabitat.com), Alex Steffen (www.alexsteffen.com), The Green Institute (www.greeninstitute.org), Mother Nature Network (www.mnn.com), John Muir College's Environmental Studies Programs (www.muir.ucsd.edu)
Singles and Style Concierge	Valerie A. Lifestyle Management (www.valeriea.com), TENFACES of She (www.tenfacesofshe.com), Daily Single (www.dailysingle.com), Hemancipation (www.hemancipation.net)
Rainbow (Gay) Concierge	Out Traveler (www.outtraveler.com), She Wired (www.shewired.com), Advocate (www.advocate.com), Gay and Lesbian Marketing Conference (www.communitymarketinginc.com), Out Professionals (www.outprofessionals.org), Passport Online (www.passportmagazine.com), The Daily Plan It, Inc. (www.thedailyplanit.info)

Checking Out the Competition

Even if you are the only concierge in town, you will probably always have competition. Who is your competition? It could be anything under the lifestyle management umbrella from professional organizers, stagers, estate sale directors, and errand-running companies to pet sitters, personal shoppers, and events management companies.

Although you might be the only concierge in town, don't forget that large concierge services have the resources to reach out and advertise all over the United States. So even though the business owner might live six states away, a larger personal concierge

On a Mission

When you're starting a business, it's very important to have a mission statement—that's a fancy term for defining your company's goals and laying out exactly how you plan to achieve those goals. There isn't a blueprint for the perfect mission statement. It's up to you to decide what you want to include. But you could use the following example to get you started.

> ACE Concierge will always put the client first. Our aim is to provide services to everyone from upscale corporate clients to busy stay-at-home moms. By virtue of our professionalism, enthusiasm, and customer service, we will become known as the foremost concierge service in Mayberry, Ohio. Our goal is to have 15 clients within our first year of business.

> As you can see, your mission statement doesn't have to be long and wordy—but it's crucial that you have one. It shows you have spent some time figuring out what type of company you want to have and what kinds of services you will offer. It also proves you're serious about your business and about establishing a good reputation.

service could still tap into business in your city. Let's face it, a company with 40 employees will be able to provide services a one-person company cannot. But if you are that one-person company, there are ways you can compete, such as giving your undivided attention to clients and being there at the drop of a hat when needed. Remember: Customer service is the name of the game.

You don't have to be all things to all people, though. As long as your clients are happy, that's what counts. Focus on providing more "personal" service to your clients; after all, that is what many of them are paying you for.

Competition is an issue you'll certainly have to address when you start your business. Some concierges we talked to believe there is enough business to go around, while

Smart Tip

One idea for a niche is to be a senior concierge who could help seniors get to and from appointments, help with home care and pet care, run errands, and do grocery shopping. Seniors may be on a limited budget, but consider marketing to their adult children. They may appreciate having a dependable person present at doctor's appointments to report back to them in detail and foot the bill.

Mission Statement Worksheet

Use this worksheet to create your own mission statement. It should include the following basic elements:

- ○ A look at the part of the concierge market your business will serve and a description of how you want the community to view your company
- ○ A look at how you want your clients to perceive your company
- ○ Where you want your business to be in one, five, and ten years

Mission Statement for_____

(Your company's name)

These are the services I want to provide, to whom, and a detailed description of what they are and are not:

_____

_____

_____

_____

_____

_____

_____

_____

_____

_____

_____

_____

_____

_____

others are nervous that, with the industry growing so quickly, competitors might soon be infringing on their territory. Two concierges recently crossed paths in a small Connecticut area and agreed to split up their territory, giving referrals to the other when appropriate. They aren't formal partners, but each helps build the other's business rather than infringe on it. You don't need to be geographically close to help each other out. Jennifer Cochran and Jackie Murphy live in different states, but often help each other review forms and advertising pieces, among other things. The internet offers a great way to "get to know" others in this growing industry even if you're not operating in the same geographic area. Jennifer is the moderator of the Yahoo! Groups Errand Services, an online forum designed to help errand runners share ideas and information. "It's not about competition. The more we work together, the more the industry is going to grow. Overall that's better for everyone. We get recognition when our industry is in the news. You can clip that *Wall Street Journal* article about the industry and put it into the sales package you deliver to your local hospital to help them see the scope of the industry and possibly contract you to provide the same service to their patients."

So what types of market research do personal concierges need to do? Most of the ones we talked to did engage in some market research. As you'll read throughout this book, each entrepreneur had to carve out his or her own niche and wing it. There really is no blueprint for this business. Those who have been around ten or more years really made their own path. Many are willing to share their secrets with you, for a fee of course, so check out the Appendix for information on getting in touch with them and pursuing your education in this exciting new field.

Some of these concierges spent time checking out their local markets and looking in online directories with Google searches and the Yellow Pages to see what types of similar services were out there. Often, they found no other businesses offering what they planned to offer, which meant the field was wide open and primed for their success. But they still needed to find out whether people were interested in what they had to offer. Some concierges sent out sales letters they designed themselves. They sent the letters to potential clients culled from business listings in the phone book or referrals from friends or family.

Today, there is a little more help for people who want to start personal concierge services. Katharine Giovanni of Triangle Concierge says she receives dozens of calls each month from people interested in starting their own services. In addition to providing concierge services, Katharine's company trains would-be concierges at its Triangle Concierge Masters Seminars or in one-on-one training sessions. Kathy S. from Elkhart took the three-day training from Triangle Concierge. She noted, "Katharine Giovanni is the guru of this industry. I was mesmerized during training."

For those who can't travel to seminar locations, they can purchase materials (such as training tools, software, must-have forms, and client management tools) or consult directly via telephone by appointment at competitive rates. The company also gives tips on various aspects of the personal concierge business, including skills for being successful, setting your fees, dealing with service vendors and commissions, and understanding legal and accounting issues. We've also provided a checklist on page 26 to give you ideas on how to start your research. You can never have too much info when it comes to marketing your business.

Just for Full-Timers?

Now, what about someone who may want to work as a personal concierge—but only on a part-time basis? Again, overwhelmingly, the concierges we talked to were full time and completely immersed in the business. But most agreed that since the business—as well as your clients—can be tailored to your specific needs and desires, you could certainly make a go of it as a part-timer. The only problem most of the concierges could foresee was that some of your clients might want you to be available full time.

But with today's technology, there is no reason you can't be available to your clients. You can give them your cell phone number, fax number, and email address where they can reach you at any time; of course, this will only work if you do your part and check your messages, faxes, and emails often. If you really want to grow your business consider texting, Tweeting (more about Tweeting in Chapter 9), and batting all correspondence back and forth immediately. Enforcing the idea that you are there for their needs and ready to perform quickly will help clients expand their idea of how helpful you can be to them. One of the most exciting things about the personal concierge business is that it really is what you make it.

How Can I Help You?

Here's a list of some of the services personal concierges can offer. Of course, with the industry growing and developing the way it is, it's impossible to give a complete list. Who knows what new service might be offered next week? But this list might help you come up with a few ideas for services you can provide to your clients.

Personal/Family Services

- Forgotten lunches/homework/ gym clothes pick up/drop off

- Interior decorating
- Landscaping
- Providing maid service

How Can I Help You?, continued

- ○ Carpet cleaning
- ○ Video store pick up/drop off
- ○ Library runs
- ○ Invitation & card writing
- ○ Pet sitting
- ○ Light housekeeping
- ○ Waiting in line at the DMV
- ○ Taking cars in for repair, oil changes, car washes
- ○ Event planning
- ○ Gift buying
- ○ Taking care of plants
- ○ Picking up dry cleaning
- ○ Doing grocery shopping
- ○ Locating hard-to-find items and collectibles
- ○ Picking up mail
- ○ Picking up meals; providing chef services
- ○ Making reservations

Luxury/VIP Services

- ○ Hotel and restaurant reservations
- ○ Meeting and event planning
- ○ Corporate and personal travel
- ○ Yacht and fishing charters
- ○ Gift baskets and floral deliveries
- ○ Executive retreats

- ○ Meet and greet at the airport for clients
- ○ Organizing itineraries for clients
- ○ Theater and entertainment tickets
- ○ Golf tournaments and tee times
- ○ Transportation
- ○ Reminder service
- ○ VIP experiences

Corporate

- ○ Personal research and special projects
- ○ Mobile notary
- ○ Making travel arrangements
- ○ Virtual assistant service
- ○ Mystery shopper for retail and restaurants
- ○ Complete expense reports

Relocation Services

- ○ Packing/unpacking
- ○ Move-in-day assistance
- ○ Home staging/decluttering/ organizing
- ○ Connecting utilities
- ○ Referring landscaping, contractors, painters, and other home improvement professionals
- ○ Change of address notification

Market Research Checklist

Need a few ideas to get you started on your market research? This list can help you get organized and coordinate your efforts.

Target Your Market

❑ Identify five markets you'd like to target.

1. _____

2. _____

3. _____

4. _____

5. _____

❑ Make a list of potential competitors offering services they'd use.

❑ Identify the weaknesses of each of those companies.

❑ Create a list of ways to make your business better than each company on that list

❑ Make calls to the businesses or individuals you've identified.

❑ Dig for data on your targeted demographic, where they are and what their incomes and median home values are. See City data (www.city-data.com) and Google Trends (www.google.com/trends) to tally up statistics.

❑ Study the services your targeted clients need. Create an online survey at www.surveymonkey.com targeted to your market to find what your market is starved for besides time.

❑ Follow up phone calls and returned surveys with thank-you notes.

❑ Schedule interviews with interested potential clients.

❑ Bring a copy of your survey to use in your interviews.

❑ Follow up interviews with thank-you notes or calls.

Research the Demographics

❑ Find out everything you can about the neighborhood, town, or county in which you wish to operate.

Market Research Checklist, continued

Research the Demographics

- ❑ Get on the internet.
- ❑ Talk to neighbors.
- ❑ Read local papers.
- ❑ Check with your local librarian.

Find Your Niche

- ❑ Choose three unique areas that will make your business stand out.

1. _____

2. _____

3. _____

Niche Development

Identifying a need and then supplying it with goods and services may seem like basic marketing, but developing a complete package of detailed, anticipated services for every one of your clients' obstacles creates a dependency, as well. All-inclusive, 110 percent offerings are a natural advantage for your concierge business because that identifies you as a time saver.

Within each specialty market is a need, waiting to be satisfied. You first need to assess your skills, and then match them to markets that are not already fulfilled in your geographic area, and finally, be all-inclusive in your service offerings. If your clients enjoy your services but have to go somewhere else for that one thing you don't offer, then it's not as convenient as it could be.

Matching Niche to You

We'll explore how to match your skills with a possible specialty niche, how to position yourself as a specialty service, and how to create a nurturing experience for your clients in this chapter. Look at the list of markets below that have very specific needs and the sample lists of services that would be of aid to their respective markets. This should get you thinking about specializing in a complete experience for your clients. This is just a small sampling of specialty concierges. There's no reason why you can't tweak these ideas, combine a few or even make up your own, based on the need in your community.

Smart Tip

Katharine Giovanni, one of the founders of the concierge industry and president and co-founder of Triangle Concierge (www.triangleconcierge.com), says that picking a very specific target market needn't be intimidating. "There are so many services you can add to your business model that if one fails, then you can just pick another idea and try again. There's no reason why you can't get paid to do something you love." All of the concierges we interviewed agreed that you should love doing whatever services you choose to offer.

Specialty Focuses

Custom assistance services run the gamut from companion animal transporter (gets your pet safely from point A to point B while you're busy moving), to new mother assistant (helps families design nurseries, find doulas, and even name their babies). New ideas are popping up daily in the form of clever businesses. We've fleshed out the offerings that fall under specific niches so you can see the wide range of ways to make yourself needed by time-challenged markets.

Relocation Concierge

There are so many things involved with the stressful process of relocating your entire life. The process begins the moment you decide to move and start your research to determine where you'll go, and it doesn't end when you land in your new spot. The process of moving is a long one and encompasses many steps from selling your house and choosing a new one to establishing new connections and stability in your new home. Think of it as closing 1,000 doors and opening 1,000 new doors. Having someone help close and open all of those doors makes it not seem so overwhelming.

It takes a long time to get settled, too, establishing your old lifestyle in new territory. The concierge that specializes in relocation needs is smart to offer services that speak to all phases of this transition. From the second the client decides to leave one life all the way up to two years after he or she has settled into the new one, there are services to be provided under the specialty of relocation. Concierges may handle a portion of cross-country relocation jobs by remote research and contracting local professionals at the arrival destination to assist. Relocation services sometimes have several teams, or contractors to divide the duties of departure, transit, and arrival.

Here are some of the many services relocation concierges provide:

- In-depth interviews to determine the needs of the client and family members, focusing on their "must have," "it would be nice," and "not a deal breaker" desires for their new home and city or town.
- Geographical research, including schools, crime statistics, political affiliations, air quality, weather averages, median income levels, average property values, etc.
- New home searches and realtor liaison services, including coordinating out-of-state trips, accommodations complete with related transportation, restaurant, temporary housing or hotel reservations, and community tours of schools, museums, and other cultural points.
- Coordinating meetings with schools, enrollment and records transfer, job searches, new employer meetings, and informational interviews with prospective new employers. Arranging introductions to any volunteerism, community involvement, sports, or other activities family members are interested in.
- Disconnecting utilities, paying final bills, notification of address changes, coordinating packing and movers, relocation travel, boarding and transferring pets, and veterinary records.
- Choosing and setting up appointments with new family doctors, veterinarians, tutors, music teachers, school board committees, and any clubs or associations of interest.
- Staging, interior design services, or just basic painting and furniture shopping for the new home, feng shui of old belongings in the new setting, and restocking the home base with staple cleaning, food, and other household necessities.

A relocation concierge may also offer corporate relocation services, which include many of the same services but for many employees, in addition to coordinating relocation expense accounts. Another option is to specialize in your own town, focusing on the second part of the move and aligning yourself with local realtors to connect with homebuyers.

Look at how these relocation concierges, or specialists, position themselves:

- Archibald Relocation (www.archibaldrelocation.com)
- Silicon Valley Relocation Specialists (www.werelocate.com)
- Corporate Concierge Bermuda (www.corporateconcierge.bm)
- 295 Park (www.295park.ch)

Google Trends (www.google.com/trends) identifies the top ten cities to conduct the search "relocation services" as: Minneapolis, MN; Charlotte, NC; Denver, CO; Cincinnati, OH; Chicago, IL; Washington DC; Miami, FL; Louisville, KY; Atlanta, GA; and Phoenix, AZ.

Eldercare Concierge

These are some of the services seniors are using either on their own, or through the care of their adult children:

- Taxi service with shopping assistance
- Shopper, cook, and light house cleaning
- Senior style/fashion consulting
- Scrap booking and assistance with memoir and legacy writing
- Family reunion organization
- Estate planning
- Video creation for memorials
- Eulogy and end-of-life direction
- Pet care
- Arthritic hand massage
- Senior matchmaking services
- Yoga and mobility therapy
- Grandparent conferences and camps

Google Trends identifies the top ten cities to conduct the search "elder care" as Boston, MA; Baltimore, MD; San Diego,

> **Tip...**
>
> **Smart Tip**
> Journalist and senior editor at www.caring.com, Barbara Repa, specializes in aging issues and provides advice to seniors such as how to prepare a list of important end-of-life questions for their families. Caring.com is just the kind of online resource that eldercare concierges should connect to for always-current awareness. Its website design and blog sections offer great examples of the kind of information and services families caring for aging parents are seeking.

CA; Austin, TX; Sacramento, CA; Tampa, FL; Philadelphia, PA; Pleasanton, CA; Reston, VA; and San Francisco, CA.

Green Concierge

From supporting their local economy by patronizing neighborhood businesses to wanting clean air and water in their homes, today's consumers are becoming more selective about where they put their money and more conscientious about what they support with their choices. They want their children to be educated in an evolved way and their companion animals to eat natural, organic foods. Many of these green consumers are becoming vegan and don't want to eat animals or purchase products tested on them. Products and services made with fair trade, sustainable practices are out there, but not so convenient to use and find all the time.

As a green concierge you may offer a service to research and shop for all of those things, like Eco Concierge (www.ecoconcierge.org) does, along with some of these additional services:

- Vegan, organic, and raw personal chef services
- Green vacation planning, using "leave no trace" travel and touring methods
- Organizing family green ethics and earth-ethical goals
- Setting up gardens, composting, and natural watering systems
- Researching and charting the course of green education for each family member
- Researching and coordinating the greenest commuter methods like www.zip car.com, www.hourcar.org, electric cars, carpooling, and cycling
- Mapping travel by bike route
- Researching and shopping for natural fiber, chemical-free carpets, furniture, and other household goods

Some businesses go ultra niche within the green category, like Kirsten Kaufman, Bike Realtor (www.bikerealtor.com). She helps bike commuters find and purchase homes along bike routes so that they can live according to their values.

Brian Mahan's Enlightened Concierge (www.enlightenedconcierge.com) is a mecca for alternative healthcare seekers, offering wellness and massage services, as well as

Stat Fact

Blue Star Families' (www.bluestarfam.org) 2010 survey of 3,634 military families determined that military families are experiencing high levels of stress. Ninety-four percent of 2009 survey respondents agreed with the statement, "The general public does not truly understand or appreciate the sacrifices made by service members and their families." Wouldn't a concierge dedicated to military families be well timed?

being a financial supporter of philanthropic endeavors. Brian likes to say that every time you get a massage through his site you are also helping someone else in need. Check out the videos on his site to see his harnessed business efforts in action, helping fund the Casa De Milagros orphanage in Peru. If green concierge is the path for you www.sustainablebusiness.com is the kind of site you should stay connected to, if not list your service on.

Business Loop Concierge

While you may not want to work for someone else as a corporate, on-site concierge, you may want to offer your services to a group of small businesses clustered in the same area of town. The things hard working nine-to-fivers don't have time to do are endless. One concierge takes full advantage of this by offering a dog walking service to a dog friendly corporation. Employees bring their dogs to work and she stops by to walk groups of four or five at once, along with taking lunch orders, picking up dry cleaning, and other errands.

Here are some additional services a business loop concierge provides:

- Pick-up and deliver laundry service
- Lunch delivery and meeting catering
- Manicures, neck and hand massage
- Cubicle feng shui and cleaning
- Plant maintenance
- Carpool driving and coordination
- Personal grocery shopping
- Appointment setting
- Gift buying
- Shoe shines and dry cleaning
- Car detailing

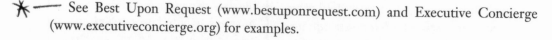 See Best Upon Request (www.bestuponrequest.com) and Executive Concierge (www.executiveconcierge.org) for examples.

Rainbow Concierge

Lifestyle management professionals to the gay community have an open field to play on, limited by only what they can do very, very well. The gay concierge service providers we looked at offered many different services, but all shared a personality profile that was stylish, sleek, and celebratory. Do those qualities describe you? Then you may be a natural for this field.

Gay weddings and unions are a rich area to specialize in because they provide opportunities to attach many additional services. Because weddings and unions are such an important milestone in people's lives, there is also the pressure of providing absolutely perfect service. That wonderful day has all eyes upon it and years of fantasy attached to it. If it's ruined by a blunder in service, there's usually hell to pay. Now, there are always ways to fix errors and create magic from mistakes, but this is not the area of service to go into if you're not a perfectionist bent on pleasing others.

Opportunities to specialize in destination selection, travel, tour and event management, under the umbrella of unions are bountiful. For a destination union you may be also providing services such as menu planning, venue décor, ceremony coordination, photography, transportation, and accommodation for visiting relatives (down to providing golf carts at the venue for old Uncle Earl who can't get around so well).

Absolute Gay Travel is a great example of one such business. It has cleverly tacked on the service, "Wine Concierge," and provide guests with an educated portfolio of Napa's hard-to-find, finest wines, shipped anywhere in the United States, (but Georgia), along with a free consultation. Guests can rent villas in Puerto Rico, Europe, Mexico, or several desirable areas of California and once they're there, many other services are offered to keep them happy. See www.absolutegaytravel.com for a good example of site presentation. Informative descriptions of travel trends, and restaurant and hotel experiences abound on Carlos Melia's Blog (www.carlosmeliablog.com).

Some of the other services you may want to offer could focus on issues same sex couples face like adoption and parenting, as well as matchmaking. Kevin Miller was sitting in a bustling restaurant catering to the gay, retired crowd in Fort Lauderdale, Florida, and noticed how many senior men were sitting alone. That shaped some of the new offerings he added to his home errand services list and before long he found himself writing singles ads for seniors in between shopping and errand running. Kevin describes one such customer, "One older gentleman in particular, wants to find a partner for companionship, but doesn't want to learn how to use computers so I set up profiles on three websites for him and because he won't type, I also respond to potential suitors for him. We get together once a week and go over print-outs of his matches."

Google Trends identifies the top three U.S. cities to conduct the search "gay tourism" as New York, NY; San Francisco, CA; and Washington, DC.

Take an Honest Look

To appropriately match yourself with your new career, you should do an honest inventory of your personality type and skills. Do you love fashion or hate wearing anything that requires more effort than a pair of Crocs, jeans, and a T-shirt? If the latter is true, you could upgrade to some nice hiking boots, a slick new Patagonia shirt, and khakis and be ready for your new life as a green concierge, provided you've got the values and interest in the subject matter. This field requires an intense curiosity in what's going on behind the scenes, ethics, and health (of the earth, animals, and humans). Are you thrifty and crafty? Do you know all the best places to shop to stretch a dollar? Can you whip up a casserole, run a carload of kids to a soccer game, and get a guest room ready for fussy in-laws? If you answered yes and love kids, animals, and the family unit, a career as a general family-oriented concierge may be more your style.

All of the concierge specialty areas require doing research but some are more hands-on than others. Ask yourself if you'd rather be dealing with people in a remote way or prefer more face-to-face contact, then look at which specialties involve dealing with customer needs when they are not at home or vice versa.

The Innovators

Researching unique personal assistant and concierge services provides a wealth of ideas for developing your specialty area. Below are some of the creative services we found ranging from whimsical and virtual to elegant and intense. Let your imagination bloom, combining the resources you bring to the table, niche types that appeal to you, and possible compatibility with your growing services list and developing profile. Try and dream up something new based on this stimulation when using the Self-Investigation Worksheet on page 38.

- *Hey Cosmo* (www.heycosmo.com) provides a variety of interesting communication services, like anonymous prank and serious phone calls that users do not want to make themselves, the delivery of emotional sound effects via phone and web, and "Blaster" phone calls to round up guests for gatherings or meetings.

- *Mumcierge* (www.mumcierge.ae) is mom service in Dubia for expatriates and natives alike, providing a one-stop-shop for anything babies and moms could need from themed coffee klatches and a reminder service to kid equipment swaps and family vacation organization.

- *Privé International* (www.priveinternational.com) caters to corporate and private clientele who are "typically high net worth individuals in business, entertainment, athletics, and politics," as defined by Privé, wishing to charter a private yacht, jet, or helicopter, hire a protection specialist (bodyguard), or book an air-conditioned safari in Kenya, among other luxury services.

- *Escort Assistant* (www.escortassistant.net) is not an escort service. It is an escorts' assistance service; a virtual concierge for escorts. It focuses on a particular caliber of escort, helping them to market their services to the right clientele, screen clients, create safety protocols, manage their schedules, check client references, provide website design, personal training, coaching, and counseling.

- *Backpacker Concierge* (www.backpackerconcierge.com) provides responsible tourism to Egypt and Jordan for clients who wish to travel in eco-tourism style while contributing to local communities and fair trade businesses. English speaking guides, connections to trusted local service providers, and 24/7 phone service are perks.

- *Green Diamond Consulting* (www.helpmegogreen.org) is an eco-lifestyle coaching service providing packages of green assessment and action plans, complete with follow-up support to help clients live with integrity and eco-wisdom. Other services include humane education, environmental consultant, yoga instruction, and Purposeful Parties coordination to help clients' friends and family learn about sustainability principles.

Where to Find Your Niche Clientele

Market research, reading lifestyle blogs, and lots of specialized sleuthing for exceptional products and services will keep you poised and quivering to supply your overtired clients with relaxation and relief. Ask yourself where your typical customer does business, works out, shops, and peruses the internet for goods and services. What do potential clients worry about and where do they go for help? What social circles do they run in and what do they do to have fun and relieve stress?

Budget some time every day to just search the internet for jewels in these areas that will connect you to your customers, as well as keep you informed of things they are interested in. Keep a bookmarked folder on your computer with resources you can advertise through, get stimulated by for blogging, and connect to your customers with. Stock your pantry with resources so that you're well informed on the things that are important to your audience and can give to their community with through social media. We'll show you how to rub shoulders with new customers via social networking in Chapter 9.

Self-Investigation Worksheet

Your assignment right now is to get out your notebook and start writing, which will help you define your plan.

List a few of your interests, talents, skills, education, and certifications.

_____

_____

_____

Now make a list of areas of frustration in your own life stimulated by not having either enough time or resources to get your own goals accomplished. Don't forget to include the challenges of your past. You may find that you have quite a long list when you combine all of the places you've been in your life and how your challenges have changed due to status in career, relationships, financial resources, or any number of other factors.

Next to each obstacle that you've listed, write down something that would have helped you at the time. With the exception of being handed a big bag of money, which is the quick answer, you'll find that there are a number of services that may have helped. Think creatively!

Frustrations, obstacles, challenges	What would have helped

4

Laying the Groundwork

This chapter will help you understand how to structure your business and give you tips on everything from naming it to finding a location for your office. Don't worry if you're the type who would rather have a root canal than deal with legal forms and zoning regulations, because we've done our best to make this relatively pain free for you.

The Name Game

Deciding what to name your business is one of the most important things you should have on your to-do list. The name you finally settle on will be what potential clients see when thumbing through the phone book, looking at your business card, or checking out an advertisement about your service.

Yes, the name should be catchy and memorable, but it should also clearly convey exactly what your business is. A very clever name that tells absolutely nothing about your business would defeat the purpose. Your goal in choosing a business name should go way beyond showing the world how creative you are.

Because customer service is a benchmark of the personal concierge business, the name of your business could play up that angle. How about something like "Gold Star Service" or "The A List"? You could also combine terms common to the concierge and hospitality industries with synonyms relating to upper-crusty society and top-notch service. Study the chart on page 41 and imagine various combinations of words from each column for a possible name for your business. If the style of concierge service you're interested in isn't represented in the Name Creator, look at www.thesaurus.com for a vast array of stimulating starter words.

Jot down key phrases and mix them up with your word combinations from the chart. Check your favorite potential names for domain availability at www.instant domainsearch.com or www.networksolutions.com.

When Abbie Allen, owner of Lifestyle Elements (http://lifestyleelements.com.au) in Torrance, Australia, was developing her name, she relied on her previous work experience, "With my marketing background, I knew it was important to have a name which would carry my business through all its different incarnations. So I tried to think about how I would like to see my business in 5, 10, 20 years and worked from there. I wanted to provide a business which serviced all the different elements in my clients' lives."

When one personal concierge was starting her business, many of her friends and family encouraged her to leave the word "concierge" out of the name, telling her she should stick with something more familiar to most people. But she rejected that advice and named her business Concierge At Large. "I knew how important it was to have the name concierge in the title," she says. "I would never have considered not having the name in the title."

A Touch of Whimsy

A current trend is to choose a more whimsical name. Examples include the Purveyors of Time in Los Angeles, California (www.purveyorsoftime.com), and The Daily Plan It, in Fort Lauderdale, Florida (www.thedailyplanit.info).

Name Creator

Words for an Upper-Echelon Concierge	Words for a Green Concierge	Neat, Quick, Time Saving Words	Household, Children, and Pets Concierge Words	Words for an Elder Concierge	Helper Words
Noble	Locavore	Flash in the pan	Whiskers	Sage	Butler
Crème de la crème	Rustic	Three Winks	Play Date	Wisdom	Caddy
Jet Set	Whole	Nanosecond	Domicile	Golden	Mate
Privileged	Earthy	Rapid	Wagging Tails	Veteran	Angel
Supreme	Robust	Crackerjack	Nest	Seasoned	Auntie
Beau Monde	Organic	Nimble	Errand	Grande	Maven
Crown	Global	On Tap	Task	Distinguished	Chum
Paramount	Conservation	Spiffy	Minutia	Ancestor	Pal
Regal	Advocate	Jiffy	Chubby Cheeks	Chieftain	Buddy
Imperial	Moss	Swift	Brass Tacks	Retiree	Sidekick
Transcendent	Willow	Lightening	Nitty Gritty	Guiding Light	Fairy Godmother
Peerless	Fair Trade	Speedy	Travails	Mature	Guy or Gal Friday
Sublime	Sustainable	Mercurial	Grindstone	Prime	Genie
Supreme	Economic	Zippy	Toil	Mellow	Magician
Sterling	Volcano	Airborne	Elbow Grease	Evolved	Accomplice
Ultimate	Ethics	Quicksilver	Daily Grind	Thriving	Butler
Elite	Bohemian	Kinetic	Chores	Mobile	Elf

Name Creator, continued

Words for an Upper-Echelon Concierge	Words for a Green Concierge	Neat, Quick, Time Saving Words	Household, Children, and Pets Concierge Words	Words for an Elder Concierge	Helper Words
Upper Crusty	Mentor	Fireball	Tender	Accomplished	Steward
Yacht Captain	Guide	Nimble	Salt Mines	Flourishing	Valet
Ivy League	Swami	Dynamic	Muscle	Fluid	Comrade
Advisor	Guru	Crafty	Moil	Domestics	Maestro
Council	Native	Savvy	Grunt Work	Pleasantries	Right Hand
Guru	Coach	Thrifty		Creature Comforts	Deputy

Others incorporate their own name in a clever way, like See Katie-Run in Walnut Creek, California, owned and operated by Katie Owensby. Jennifer Ferri runs The Ferri Godmother in Middlefield, Connecticut. A Load Off concierge in Suffolk, Virginia, has a name that speaks for itself, and its URL can't be beaten (www. whataloadoff.com)!

Some choose whimsical names because they have a special meaning to them. Jennifer Cochran of Warp Speed Errands chose her name because, "I'm a huge Star Trek fan. Warp speed is the speed that ships travel in space [on the TV show], so it just fit. It came to me in an epiphany. I run errands fast, so 'Warp Speed' works."

Right Where You Are

Some business owners like to incorporate the name of their town or a distinctive feature of the area when naming their business. Kellye Garrett of Cowtown Concierge Services (www. cowtownconcierge.com) named her business

Smart Tip

Tip...

Try Wordlab's free Business Name Generator widget (www.wordlab.com). Catchy monikers like Silver Victor Services, Whizbang Works, Lamplighter, Running Doodlebug, Playground, Inc., and Bliss Factory are churned out for the taking. Don't forget to check with your county clerk's office to see if your name is already registered as a fictitious or assumed business name in your area.

after the nickname for her hometown of Ft. Worth, Texas. Concierge by the Sea operates in the coastal community of Lewes, Delaware.

Using concierge in the title paired with a geographic indicator makes a simple name and could work well in this industry. One personal concierge said it was "a complete no-brainer" when it came to naming her business. "We live in an area that has three main cities and the area is known as the Triangle," she says. "So when it came time to name our business we just had to go with the name Triangle Concierge. Nothing else would have made sense. It says where we're from and what we do."

Put your thinking cap on, use your imagination, and remember that some of your best options for a business name are familiar features, places, or ideas. Enlist family and friends to help you come up with the perfect name. Have a small group over for a casual dinner and toss around some names to see what kinds of reactions you get. If your creativity needs a jump-start, take a look at the personal concierge services in the Appendix. Sorry, you can't borrow any of those names for your business, but the bright ideas should provide some wonderful inspiration for you. You can also use the worksheet we've provided on page 46 to help get you going.

Of course, you should definitely consider whether the name or the initials of the business have a double meaning. For instance, make sure the initials don't spell out something inappropriate or something that could be misconstrued. On the other hand, perhaps the initials spell out a slogan for your new business. For example, Associated Concierge Experts would have the initials ACE. Therefore, you could bill yourself as an "ace concierge."

Making It Official

Since you want the name of your business to be unique and avoid problems with other business owners, you must do a trademark search to ensure no one else is using either the same or even a similar name, especially

> **Bright Idea**
> Some enterprising business owners purposely choose a name for their business that begins with the letter "A" so it will come first in phone books and other lists.

in your industry. Word search the names of your geographic area, plus your name idea and then just do a search on the name alone to make sure no one has used it in another part of the United States. Even if there is a business out there whose name is similar, it can cause confusion to potential clients. You may think fielding calls from people who intended to call someone else can be a good thing, because they're exposed to your business, but the down side is that the business owner who worked hard to choose a unique name could sue you. Make sure you check the United States Patent and Trademark Office as a final step at www.uspto.gov. While it's impossible to be 100 percent sure that your name is unique, this will at least let you know who's officially registered theirs and avoid competition in your area.

Once you have a name picked out, the next step is to register it as your dba (doing business as), or "fictitious business name." This is usually a fairly simple procedure that ensures someone else isn't already using the name you've chosen. If nobody else is using it, you may pay a fee to register the name as yours. If someone else already has dibs on the name, you can move to the next name on your list.

The procedure to register a name can vary depending on where you live. In some states, it's as simple as visiting the county clerk's office, while in other states you may need to check in with the office of the secretary of state.

In any case, it's generally not a time-consuming procedure and usually involves nothing more than filling out a registration form, paying a registration fee, and turning in a form from your local newspaper that shows you have advertised your fictitious business name. Registration fees are usually inexpensive, although fees can vary by state and region.

Structure Is Good

Now that your business has a name, it needs a structure. You have the option of operating your new business as a sole proprietorship, an LLC (a Limited Liability Company), a partnership, or corporation.

The Sole Proprietor

A sole proprietorship is an option if you have no partners. The set up is extremely simple. In most towns you don't need to fill out specific paperwork to declare your business a sole proprietorship. (You of course need to fill out other paperwork to get things like a business license and a dba certificate, but not to specifically form a sole proprietorship). But the downside is that your personal assets aren't protected if your business is sued. So, if you have an employee running errands and that employee hits a pedestrian, you as the business owner may lose business and personal assets if a judgment is placed against your sole proprietorship. That means depending on the size of the judgment and the kind of liability insurance you have, you could lose your home, your kid's college funds, and the like.

A Limited Liability Company

An LLC is similar to a sole proprietorship, but offers a legal way to keep your personal assets separate from your business obligations. It offers protection of your home, your bank accounts, and other assets in the event that your business experiences an unforeseen tragedy. As the name suggests, it limits your liability in a tough financial situation.

Choosing Partnerships

Most personal concierges that were interviewed for this book set up their businesses as sole proprietorships or LLCs, but you may want to go a different route. It's important to look at all of your options so you can determine the best choice for your own situation.

Cynthia A., the personal concierge from San Diego, structured her business as a partnership and says it works like a charm because she found the right partners. "I have two partners, and we just function so well together that everything runs almost perfectly," she says. "One of us is good at one area of the business, while the others are good in other areas. It's a great balance. As far as the legal aspects of a partnership, I'd definitely advise anyone to go through an attorney because there are complicated aspects to it and there is a lot of paperwork. As for the emotional aspects or the rewards, I think that when you have a partnership, everyone puts equal effort into the business and each person cares about it as much as the others. That's how it should work, anyway."

> ### Bright Idea
> Start a file for your business associates' contact information. Organize it by business type or profession for easy use. That way, when you need to call your attorney, accountant, or a new client, the number is at your fingertips. Try Sage ACT! 2011 software packages to utilize easy crossover from your cell phone, Facebook or LinkedIn accounts, and email, just to mention a few. Its ability to save and remind you of where you left off in communication with a client or vendor is very handy. It coordinates phone calls, emails, and other correspondence with contact information. See www.act.com for details.

A Corporation

Most personal concierges qualify to become S Corporations, which means they can structure their business as a corporation, but avoid some of the tax consequences

45

Business Name Worksheet

List five business name ideas associated with the type of service you plan to provide as a personal concierge. For instance: professional, efficient, detailed.

1. _____

2. _____

3. _____

4. _____

5. _____

List five business name ideas based on the region of the country where you live. You can use the name of your town or state, for example. Think about something your area is known for. Remember Cowtown Concierge and North Coast Concierge we talked about? Have fun with it.

1. _____

2. _____

3. _____

4. _____

5. _____

List five business names that are clever or whimsical. Remember to consider the types of services, and image you're trying to communicate to prospective clients. Use your imagination.

1. _____

2. _____

3. _____

4. _____

5. _____

Business Name Worksheet, continued

OK, you've spent some time narrowing down your choices. You think you've decided which name is right for you. Now you need to:

○ Write it out one more time for good measure and then take a look at the initials; make sure they don't spell out something inappropriate. Say it out loud to hear what it sounds like. Run the name by family and friends to see if they're as impressed with it as you are.

○ Check out the website address to make sure it's available.

○ Check with your county clerk's office to make sure the name isn't already in use.

○ Consult your local directory listings, online, and in the Yellow Pages to ensure another business doesn't have the same or similar name.

○ Check the United States Patent and Trademark Office to see if anyone else has registered your name at www.uspto.gov.

○ Let everyone know that you've officially named your new business!

---

of a standard C corporation. With a standard corporation, the corporation pays tax, then the shareholders (in this case you) pay tax on what the corporation pays you (your salary); in effect you pay taxes twice as a standard C Corporation. To be an S Corporation, you need fewer than 100 shareholders and meet a few different criteria.

More Than a Cubicle

It's a fact that you will need an office, whether it's located in your home or elsewhere. There are plenty of choices available for your office setup—executive suites, home offices, and alternative offices (such as sharing office space with another professional). We'll take a look at some of those choices in this section.

No matter where your office is located, it's important that your clients get a good impression when dealing with you. That first impression is very important because it might make or break their relationship with you. This means considering not only what the neighborhood looks like and what it says about your business, but also whether your location is easy to reach.

Home Sweet Office

If you decide to have a homebased office, you can locate it anywhere in your home that works for you. Take a look at the worksheet we have given you on page 51 to help you with these decisions. Several of the personal concierges we talked to started out with home businesses. One located her office in the basement, another set hers up in a spare bedroom, and another was lucky enough to have a large room in her home designed to be an office.

Some people locate their office in a den, garage, corner of the kitchen or dining room, or even in a closet! Sure, that option wouldn't work for long if your business grew rapidly or if you had a need for employees. But in the beginning, if you had nowhere

> **Tip...**
>
> ### Smart Tip
>
> If you decide to have a home office, you'll probably want to set some ground rules for friends and family. Make sure they realize that just because you're working from home, you're not available to run errands for them during the day or to baby-sit on a moment's notice. Let them know that during working hours, you're working! They'll respect you for being upfront, and you'll be able to focus on your job.

else to put your computer, you could clear out a closet, turn a box upside down, set up your computer, and go to work. The best thing about it is that nobody ever has to know your office is in a closet because when company comes over, all you have to do is shut the door—and voilà! The office is hidden.

No Need for the Tax Man Blues

Some personal concierges will tell you there is one great advantage to having a homebased business: You can write some expenses off your income taxes. If you are using even a portion of your home for an office, the IRS will allow you to write off some costs as a home business deduction. You are allowed to claim that deduction if—and only if—you are using that space solely for an office. If you're using the space for other things as well, you can't claim it as a deduction. You can get information from the IRS about tax deductions for homebased businesses by visiting www.irs.gov.

Rules and Regulations

You'll need to learn about your local zoning regulations if you decide to locate your office in your home. The personal concierge business isn't the type of business in which you'd have clients visiting your office, so you should not have to worry about parking restrictions or annoyed neighbors. But you should still make a call to your local county clerk's office and ask whether any permits are needed.

While you're on the phone, go ahead and inquire about a business license, if you haven't already. Since you've come this far, you want to make sure you have all of your t's crossed and your i's dotted.

Growth Spurt

You may find that you eventually have to make the jump from a homebased business to an office away from home. Although many of the personal concierges we interviewed did indeed have home businesses, others who had started at home had been forced to move when their businesses began growing.

One of the concierges we talked to had started her business in a corner of her dining room; another located hers in a spare bedroom. Valerie Fidan of Valerie A. Lifestyle Management in Belmont, California, feels the biggest mistake entrepreneurs make when they are starting out a business is renting an office space in trying to make their not quite operating business look like it's fully underway. She points out that the because the business is not yet bringing in revenue, it's a waste of money and it's more logical to spend on methods that bring customers in, rather than on how things look once they are in.

Most of our concierges agreed that it's fine to keep your office at home until you have a few employees and are bringing in enough money to justify renting, but keeping that home office completely separate from the machining of your personal home life is mandatory if you want to get anything done. Loreine G. points out two things to consider before running your business from home, "Prepare yourself for a complete lack of structure. There is no boss to tell you

Bright Idea

How about a completely free, quiet office, complete with all the resource materials you need to be a never-ending resource of bright ideas for your clients? Many libraries have private study rooms, quiet corners to work in, and a free wifi connection. All it takes is a little discipline to make the free library office idea work for you. Choose a branch close to your house so you can walk and talk on your way. Beginning and ending your day with fresh air and a walk is a good way to decompress and stay fresh. Spend the first hour of your day making callbacks before you get to the library. When you get there, get caught up on email correspondence and scheduling. Now comes the fun part—search the stacks of knowledge for fodder for your client newsletter, blog, and service perks. In Chapter 9 we'll show you how to use all of the great ideas you find for your social media profile and e-tools. You can always step outside the library to take and make phone calls if you need to and it's a great way to start your day before the barrage of errands you no doubt have scheduled for your time-challenged clients.

Change of Heart

When Katharine G. decided to start her personal concierge service, she knew her business would not be homebased. "I used to have an event-planning business," she says. "I ran it out of my basement and for a variety of reasons, it just was not working. It wasn't going well at all."

The next time she upgraded, Katharine spent considerable time researching different locations and ended up with office space in a corporate building. Because her business has employees, she needed a larger office than she could find at home anyway.

She says concierges who are looking for office space should leave no stone unturned. "Talk to everyone you know because they might have a friend of a friend of a friend who is about to move out of their office space and it could be just the right office for you."

when to get up, so it is imperative that you treat your home office like any other office and maintain a disciplined schedule.

When you think about it, a homebased business can quickly take over your life in terms of paperwork, files, phone calls at all hours, dogs barking, FedEx deliveries on a daily basis, faxes, mail, etc.

If you do decide to start looking for an office away from home, the options are endless. You can look into sharing an office with another businessperson or check out corporate office spaces that may be underutilized and are offering good deals on rent. You can also check out other options, including renting a house or an apartment for your business. Remember, what you need is space and not a fancy address since, more than likely, your clients won't visit your office very often—if ever.

Some entrepreneurs lease space over storefronts. If you do find such a space, make sure the storefront is one you won't mind sharing space with and not one that could hurt your image. Some concierges report having very good luck locating their offices in business parks or busy corporate areas because of the networking possibilities. None of them seemed too hip on locating

Smart Tip

One call—or sometimes two—can do it all. Just call the state and local government offices in your area to find out what permits are required for your business.

their offices near busy shopping centers, though, because these places lacked the business image they were aiming to project.

But you can decide on these issues for yourself because every town and city is different, and what works for one person might not work for you. By the same token, what didn't work for someone else might work perfectly for you!

We've covered all of the important factors involved in laying the groundwork for your business. The structures, fees, and licenses mentioned should be the main ones you'll have to consider. The more information you have, the better prepared you will be for your new business venture. You can never have too much good information.

Home Office Location Worksheet

Use this handy worksheet to pick the best place in your home for an office.
Name four possible office locations in your home.

1. _____

2. _____

3. _____

4. _____

Make a list of the pros and cons of each location.

1. What is the lighting situation? Do you think you'd have adequate lighting? If not, can anything be done to change that?

_____

_____

_____

_____

_____

_____

_____

Home Office Location Worksheet, continued

2. Is there room to set up your computer and any other supplies you might need?

_____

_____

_____

3. What about noise? Will you be able to concentrate or are you right next to a window where you'd have to listen to a leaf blower for an hour every morning?

_____

_____

_____

4. Are there adequate phone and electrical outlets? How frustrating it would be to get everything set up and then realize you don't have phone or electrical outlets within reach.

_____

_____

_____

Money Is No Obstacle

In this chapter, we come face to face with the costs involved in starting a personal concierge service. Don't worry, it's not as scary as it sounds. We've provided a list of items you need to properly equip your office, and given a rundown of the operating expenses you can expect to encounter. You'll find sample worksheets for figuring your startup costs as well as your monthly income and operating expenses. With a little ingenuity, you won't have to break the bank.

Startup Costs

It's time to get down to the nitty-gritty of just how much it costs to get your business up and running. One of the best things about establishing a personal concierge business is that the startup costs can be minimal. That benefit is one we heard about over and over again from personal concierges. The low startup costs were one of the things that attracted them to the business in the first place. Many started running their business from home with around $500 and equipment they already had, such as computers and telephones. Some started with nothing and got by using their cell phones and laptops for 100 percent digital communication, advertising, and social marketing. They found free ways to create a web and office presence and did their own shopping to find very inexpensive business card and other hard copy collateral deals.

Since you won't have to purchase inventory, your biggest expenses aside from office equipment could be for advertising, business cards, stationery, and website design.

Here's a rundown of what you may need to get your business off to a roaring start:

- A good computer system with a modem, CD or DVD burner, and printer. Most libraries have free wifi and computers that you can use before you get your own, but receiving faxes there is most often not an option. Another option is to just run your communications strictly paper-free and skip the fax and printer. Some customers appreciate having everything sent through email, but there will be times when you may want to print out travel confirmations or directions for a harried client and a printer is vital.
- Software for accounting and contact management
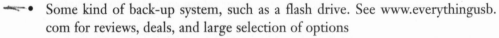
- Some kind of back-up system, such as a flash drive. See www.everythingusb. com for reviews, deals, and large selection of options
- Fax machine or service
- Scanner (consider an all-in-one device printer/fax/scanner)
- Phone with two or three lines and caller ID
- Answering machine or voice mail
- Cellular phone (preferably a smartphone with email capability, like a Treo or BlackBerry, for example)
- Personal Digital Assistant (PDA) such as a Palm device
- Office supplies and stationery, including business cards
- High-speed internet access (DSL, cable, or satellite)

- Website (including hosting, design, and implementation)
- Insurance
- Legal and accounting services
- Startup advertising

You may already have most of the basic office equipment. Of course, if you're one of those lucky people for whom money is no object, you can add all sorts of extras to your office: file cabinets, bookshelves, comfortable chairs, a copier, and anything else your heart desires. We've provided a checklist of equipment you'll need to get up and running on page 69.

> **Bright Idea**
>
> Cynthia A., the personal concierge in San Diego, says even when she's not at work, she's often thinking about work—and about her clients. "If I'm driving and I spot a new restaurant, entertainment venue, bakery, or something like that, I always make note of it because it might be useful in the future," she says. "I'm constantly asking questions and thinking about the marketing of my business."

If you're like most folks starting a new business, you are really watching your budget and don't want to spend a penny more than you have to. If you're really scrimping, you can find many ways to cut corners. Remember, your clients never have to see your home office, so if you don't have the funds to buy a computer desk, no problem! Set up the computer on your kitchen counter or dining room table. Do your best to keep it as separate as possible from the rest of your home to stay as productive as possible.

Getting Equipped

Startup expenses for your business will vary depending on factors such as your office location, how much equipment you need to buy, and how much startup capital you have at your disposal. (See the worksheet on page 60 for examples). Use the worksheet on page 61 to come up with your own official startup figure.

Computer Choices

You and your computer are going to be spending a lot of time together, for everything from keeping track of your clients' requests to generating invoices and taking care of accounting. So, you need to find a computer that can meet the needs of your business. How do you decide which is the best one for you? Research what's out there by reading product reviews and talking to computer experts, then do some comparison-shopping.

Choose from two basic operating systems, Windows and Mac. Both systems have their critics and their proponents, so if you already have a favorite, feel free to stick with it. Popular belief in the past has been that most business software has and will continue to be developed primarily for Windows, but there are so many expert opinions these days that express otherwise and sing the praises of the intuitive, less hassle design of Macs. Technology author, geek, and TV show host, Chris Pirillo posted a great article on his site arguing this point. View the article

Smart Tip

Before you go computer shopping, jot down a short list of what you want your system to do. It will save you some time and make your trek to the computer store a lot easier.

here: www.chris.pirillo.com/50-reasons-to-switch-from-microsoft-windows-to-apples-mac-os-x/. A more technical article that sifts through the features of both can be viewed here and is suggested reading before you make your decision: www.wisegeek.com/should-i-buy-a-mac-or-a-pc.htm.

To be able to take full advantage of internet capabilities, as well as store files and run various programs, you should make sure that your computer has at least 1 GB processor, 1GB to 2MB RAM, plus at least a 60GB hard drive and a CD/DVD drive. You should also make sure you have an Ethernet port and several USB connections to install peripherals, such as your printer, scanner, speakers, flash drives, and a camera.

Be prepared to pay from $800 to $2,000 for a good computer system, including a printer. Remember, a desktop machine will be cheaper than a laptop or notebook computer with the same system specifications, but it's not the handiest option. Laptops are great for in-person customer interviews and showing custom slideshows and presentations to your customers. iBooks come with very user-friendly software to make your own movies, (complete with custom soundtracks), take impromptu photos, and burn DVDs, among other things. Check out sales at local stores (Best Buy, CompUSA, and Circuit City), warehouse stores (Sam's Club and Costco), and direct manufacturers (www.dell.com, www.apple.com, or www.gateway.com). Also scour the internet for package deals and sales. Slow growth and upgrading equipment by those first few high

rolling customers can be extra incentive to just focus on outstanding customer service and drumming up new clients in the beginning. Many entrepreneurs wait until they land that really profitable first customer to purchase the bigger ticket items. Sometimes it's best to just make do with what you have until you can fund the right equipment. You can stick with the computer you have or buy a simple system for now and upgrade later. Choose a high-powered desktop now and add a middle-of-the-road laptop later, for example.

Dollar Stretcher

If your budget is really tight, consider contacting a locally owned computer store to build you a system from scratch. Often these systems can save you 30 percent or more. They work just as well, without the big budget advertising and branded stickers on the side. Plus you know who to take it to if you have any trouble.

Flashing Your Clients

What is a USB flash drive? Well, basically, it's a device that allows you to quickly copy material from your hard drive onto a portable disk drive. Why do you need a USB flash drive? Consider this: You've just updated your computer files, which now include information on 30 potential clients, some recent market-research data, and a couple of files you plan to use in a new promotional brochure. What happens if your computer crashes or gets stolen? The answer is simple but frightening: You would lose all of that hard work. But if you have a USB flash drive, you can copy important files onto it and store the drive in a separate place. That way, if something happens to your computer, you'll have a solid backup.

Flash drives range in size from 32MB up to 64GB. You can obtain a 1 to 4 GB USB flash drive from $8 to $40. Check www.amazon.com for new and used deals on these. The cost for backing up your company data is priceless. Keep an extra on

Dollar Stretcher

Many companies purchase USB flash drives in bulk, slap their logo on them, load them up with product documentation, and ship them off to individual clients. If you're lucky enough to receive one of these giveaways, don't simply toss it once you've read the marketing material. Instead, dump the files and use the drive for your own purposes.

A Word about Wireless

Wireless computing devices are already as commonplace today as cell phones were ten years ago, and that shows no sign of stopping anytime soon. If you can afford to buy a laptop, do so, especially if you have a home office. Make sure that it has a wireless modem built in. You can conduct business meetings with full access to your files at a client's office, at a hotel, or wherever you need to. Many coffee shops and cafes have free wireless internet access for their customers. You can meet your clients there or at a virtual office, which does everything from renting out meeting rooms and serving coffee to providing professional receptionist service and a fancy address for your reputation. See www.cornerofficeinc.com, www.davincivirtual.com, and www.virtualoffice.com to understand how virtual office features can work for you. Most hotels also have wireless internet access on their property, which is great if you're onsite planning an event and need to access the internet or send a quick email. Once you have a computer with wireless internet access, you'll be surprised you lived without it.

Book It!

Make sure your brain is as well equipped as your office. When it comes to checking out the written word regarding your new business venture, you should plan on becoming a real bookworm. Visit bookstores and libraries and take a look at online bookstores. There is a listing of helpful books in the Appendix at the back of this book, but here are a few more titles you may want to get your hands on.

○ *Thank You Very Much: A Book for Anyone Who Has Ever Said, "May I Help You?"* (Ten Speed Press), Holly Stiel

○ *Inbound Marketing: Get Found Using Google, Social Media and Blogs* (John Wiley and Sons), David Meerman Scott and Brian Halligan

○ *Start Your Own Business: The Only Startup Book You'll Ever Need*, 5th Edition (Entrepreneur Media), by the staff of Entrepreneur Media

○ *Influence: The Psychology of Persuasion* (Collins Business Essentials), Robert B. Cialdini, Ph.D.

○ *The New Rules of Marketing and PR: How to Use Social Media, Blogs, News Releases, Online Video, and Viral Marketing to Reach Buyers Directly* (John Wiley and Sons), David Meerman Scott

○ *The Thank You Economy* (HarperCollins), Gary Vaynerchuk

○ *Going Above and Beyond: Reach the Pinnacle of Customer Service by Learning How to . . . Think and Act Like a Concierge* (NewRoad), Katharine C. Giovanni

○ *Getting Things Done: How to Achieve Stress-free Productivity* (Penguin), David Allen

○ *The Housewife's Handbook: How to Run the Modern Home* (Bloomsbury), Rachel Simhon

Don't wait for a rainy day to surf the internet or get caught up on research reading. Develop a habit of either starting or ending your workday with a good half hour of it with a nice cup of tea. It's a stimulating way to keep your creativity bubbling and remain a source of cutting edge information for your customers' convenience.

hand for taking proposals from your computer to the print shop quickly and easily. Check out the ClickFree Automatic Backup Drive by Storage Appliance Corp. for $130 at www.clickfree.com. This nifty gadget does automatic backups of updated files and makes the whole process easier by not requiring software and allowing you to backup multiple PC and Mac computers on it.

The Fine Print

New printer models are coming out every day, and there are some great choices out there. You can find a decent inkjet printer for under $150. But if you plan to design your own brochures and marketing materials, you might consider a laser printer in the $500 range.

Again, you'll want to shop around. Don't forget to factor in the cost of ink. A single inkjet print cartridge can run between $20 and $40, so if you do a lot of printing it can definitely add up.

These days with the planet becoming more conscientious about waste, more businesses are going paperless. It's nice to have a business card to hand out at gatherings, but most of the concierges we talked to didn't do much printing, even for billing, using mostly digital, email notices for their clients. You could get away with getting your cards and stationery printed through inexpensive online printers such as www.vistaprint.com and www.123print.com for as little as $10, delivery included.

Many different companies offer printing services, so don't feel like you have to splurge on an expensive printer right away. FedEx Kinkos (www.fedex.com) allows you to print right from your word processing program (like Microsoft Word) directly to a store near you, with its File, Print, FedEx Kinko's software. In fact, if you're shipping the item you're printing, they can do it all for you while you sit in your cozy office. No need to even physically deliver the file.

> **Dollar Stretcher**
> You're probably going to be purchasing printer/copier/fax paper in bulk, so make sure to ask the store you patronize if you can get a discount. Most storeowners will be more than happy to do so because it guarantees a repeat customer who may spread the word about the store's policy.

Just the Fax

Sure, you can get by without a fax machine or service. But it would probably be to your advantage to have one because your clients will really appreciate it. Say you're

Startup Expenses

Here's a list of startup expenses for two hypothetical personal concierge services. The first is a one-person, homebased business called ACE Concierge. The business owner already has a personal computer and some of the basic office equipment he will need. First Class Concierge, on the other hand, is based out of a commercial office space, and has one full-time employee. The owner of First Class decided to invest in a new computer system, a deluxe website, and a large initial advertising campaign. Neither owner draws a salary; instead, they take a percentage of their net profits as income.

Expenses	ACE	First Class
Rent and utilities (deposit and first month)	N/A	$1,700
Office equipment and supplies	$750	$3,000
Phone system (including voice mail and cell phone)	$200	$300
Employee payroll and benefits	N/A	$1,800
Licenses	$150	$150
Insurance (first six months)	$500	$1,000
Internet access (DSL, set-up and first month)	$70	$130
Website design	$300	$4,000
Legal and accounting services	$150	$500
Startup advertising	$500	$1,000
Rolodex or little black book	(Priceless)	(Priceless)
Memberships	$500	$5,000
Miscellaneous (add 10% of Total)	$320	$1,905
Total Startup Costs	**$3,520**	**$20,955**

Startup Expenses Worksheet

Use this worksheet to calculate your own startup costs. If you decide on a home-based office, you won't need to worry about rent or employee expenses.

Expenses	
Rent and utilities (deposit and first month)	$
Office equipment and supplies	
Phone system (including voice mail and cell phone)	
Employee payroll and benefits	
Licenses	
Insurance (first six months)	
Internet access	
Website design	
Legal and accounting services	
Startup advertising	
Miscellaneous (add 10% of Total)	
Official Startup Figure	$

working on getting some price quotes for a cruise for one client and running down costs for a 50th anniversary party for another client. Instead of putting the quotes in the mail or leaving the info on an answering machine, you could just fax the information to your clients, guaranteeing that they would have it in minutes. Saving time and money on postage.

These days a big clunky fax machine may seem like a relic (or at a minimum, an expensive door stop). But just a few short years ago, most business (even those which were homebased) had a fax machine. Your other option is a fax service. You can create documents on your computer, and then send them to a clients' fax machine (or their fax service) instantly. If they have a traditional fax machine, they'll receive the hard copy, black and white document they expect to see, never suspecting that you "faxed" it virtually. If they have a service, they can likely view their document on their computer then print it as they wish. Check out a service like eFax (www.efax.com) that has a basic, inexpensive service to get you started. If you're looking for the ability to edit and manipulate the text in the faxes you receive, take a look at its eFax Pro service for a small monthly fee.

Dollar Stretcher

Don't be too quick to buy a freestanding fax machine. If you're using a suite of office productivity software (meaning programs with word processing, spreadsheet, and database programs like Microsoft Office), you likely can set your system up to fax directly from your documents. Look in your Help information to see the steps that work for your system.

If you choose to go the route of freestanding fax machine rather than service, we recommend a combination unit that's a fax/copier/printer/scanner. Again, plan to shop around and take your time finding just the right machine for you. Prices range from $130 to $600 for multifunction fax machines.

Line One Is for You

We'll just take it for granted that you already have a phone line in your home. But if you're going to base your business at home, it really is necessary to go ahead and get a second line. Why? The best scenario is to have one line for personal use and a second line for business use. If you insist on having an actual fax machine, consider getting a third line specifically for it. Remember that the fax service eliminates this expense.

It's also a good idea to have a two-line phone for your business so you can put one caller on hold while you answer a second line. This way, if you're on the phone and a call is coming in, you won't miss that important call you've been waiting for.

Some entrepreneurs like to have speakerphones so they can attend to other things while talking to their clients. But be forewarned that some people don't like their calls being broadcast on speakerphones. If you plan to use a speakerphone while

Dollar Stretcher

Why pay a long-distance fee if you can call your vendors on their toll-free number? When a vendor signs a contract, make it a point to ask if the company has a toll-free number. The savings add up!

talking to clients, ask them ahead of time if it's OK. A good speakerphone, equipped with two lines, auto redial, mute button, memory dial, and other features, ranges from about $50 to $150. Shop around and look for sales and other specials, and you can sometimes get a better deal.

Concierges with a lot of out-of-town clients say toll-free numbers are a must for them so their clients can always get in touch with them without any long distance charges. Those concierges who serve mostly in-town clients don't see a need for a toll-free number. This is one more case where you will need to make that decision based on your business, your volume of calls, and whether you have a lot of out-of-town clients.

> **Dollar Stretcher**
>
> When you are starting your business and trying to watch every single penny, you should think about bartering as a way to save on startup advertising costs. Perhaps you can trade some of your services in exchange for advertising your new business.

Don't Miss a Call

It's important to make sure you receive all of your incoming calls even if you aren't there to take them yourself. To make sure you get all your messages, you'll need to have either an answering machine or voice mail. We recommend voice mail, so every call is answered and clients never get a busy signal. If some natural disaster strikes and you find yourself without power, your voice mail may still work, while an answering machine likely won't.

Just like an answering machine, voice mail takes your messages when you can't be in the office. Voice mail costs vary depending on which features you choose, but basic voice mail service from your local phone company generally runs in the neighborhood of $6 to $10 per month. Try business voice mail services accessible by phone, email, or online at www.ringcentral.com, starting at $9.99 per month.

Whatever you do, make sure you have something in place to handle those all-important calls that are sure to come in the second you step out of the office. The worst thing that can happen when a client calls you is for the phone to just ring and ring. If clients get that kind of reception on their first call, they might never make a second call. You don't want that to happen! With a new business, every client counts. Try to avoid using a cutesy script on your answering machine or voicemail message. These will only make you look unprofessional.

Cellular Phones and Other Gadgets

Every concierge we talked to said they wouldn't dream of being without their cellular phone. Sure, your clients can leave a message on your answering machine

▲

> **Smart Tip** *Tip...*
>
> Find out if the phone company you're using offers features like call forwarding. You can forward your business line to your cell phone, so you never miss a call while you're on the go.

or send you an email. But what about those clients who want something handled yesterday? If they can't reach you, they may turn to someone else.

With the increase in popularity of cellular phones, most companies are literally giving phones away with a two-year service agreement. Full functioning smartphones, like the BlackBerry or the Treo, will set you back $200 to $300 with a two-year service agreement. With a smartphone you have instant access to receive and send email from anywhere you have a phone service. Most smartphones allow you the ability to make and receive phone calls, conduct internet searches, manage your schedule, manage email, use some office software (like viewing and editing documents and spreadsheets), take photos and video, record voice memos, and listen to music, all from a single device. For a professional who needs to be ready at all times to fill a need, it's not a luxury. It's a necessity.

If you choose not to get a smartphone, make sure you keep a PDA (or personal digital assistant) that you can quickly synchronize with your computer, to keep your schedule at your fingertips wherever you go.

The expense of a cellular phone can vary widely depending on usage and your service plan. For instance, if you talk in the neighborhood of 450 minutes a month (or around 15 minutes a day), you could pay as little as $40 per month, but if you talk 6,000 minutes a month (roughly 3 hours a day), you might spend $70 per month.

If you add a data package to get email, it's around an additional $40 per month. Make sure you read the fine print. Many companies allow you to talk to their other customers for free, not using any minutes out of your pool of minutes, or they let you choose five to ten numbers to call for free. There are literally hundreds of options, so look for the plan that fits you and your business best.

The Software Scene

Most of the personal concierges we talked to say that they don't need fancy software programs because their work mostly involves dealing with clients one-on-one, tracking down hard-to-find items, or

> **Smart Tip** *Tip...*
>
> If you're looking for an upgrade to standard voice mail, consider using a virtual receptionist service like eVoice Receptionist. eVoice answers the phone when you can't, transfers them to one of your extensions (home, business, cell, as you see fit), then sends voicemails to you as email attachments. All for the low price of $12.95 a month.

making arrangements by phone. However, some of them did splurge on accounting software programs. Others took the plunge and purchased software programs specifically designed for payroll concerns. But if you are going to operate a one-person, homebased business, you won't have to deal with payroll issues and your accounting concerns will be minimal.

Still, software programs abound, and since you are going to be shopping for computers, printers, fax machines, etc., you might as well take a look at the software, too. You might come across the perfect piece of software to make your day-to-day business life easier. Most personal concierges use Intuit QuickBooks, Quicken, or similar programs for keeping track of finances and generating invoices. Others find someone to take care of those needs for them. For your own business, it will depend on how big a client list you have and whether you can find a software program that keeps you from drowning in financial paperwork.

Internet Access

Use the internet as your superhighway to higher education. Information on every topic you could possibly imagine and unexpected education sources are around every corner online. Often you'll be searching for one thing and inadvertently find a fantastic idea for something else. With dedicated, focused, habitual searching, you can become a walking encyclopedia of everything your customers need. More ways to use the internet are discussed in Chapter 9. Check out the Appendix for information on great online groups for the aspiring personal concierge.

The cost of internet access is surprisingly low and sometimes free, depending on where you live and work. We recommend using the highest speed internet connection available in your area. National Broadband Map helps find the fastest connection providers in your area to help you make that choice. See www.broadbandmap.gov for high-speed connection service for cable and DSL. Both high-speed connections require a special modem to process the signal coming into your home, and then connect to your computer. In most cases, the company will give you the modem for free. If they don't offer it, ask. Contact your phone company, satellite TV, or cable TV provider for services and prices in your area.

If you live near any kind of metropolis at all, excluding some Podunk towns that haven't caught up with the times, you are most likely near a wireless network. If you've got wireless capabilities in your laptop you can pick up on a free wireless connection at libraries, airports, and many types of businesses including cafes. For the price of a cup of coffee you can connect daily in wifi cafes. Many cities have free public wifi that only requires registering to gain access to. Apple iBooks and iPhones have built in network sensors that show you all of your wifi options in each area you rove to. This is great for people who run all over town and live on their computers or phones. Be careful of "piggybacking," though. If your system picks up on a private connection without a password, you may not know it and be unwittingly sending information into an unsecured network.

If high-speed connections aren't available in your area, a slightly cheaper, but much less effective, option is to choose a dial-up ISP (Internet Service Provider) like PeoplePC, NetZero, or ATT Yahoo! Dial-up Service. It works anywhere you can find a phone line, but it works slowly. As more sites on the internet take advantage of graphic-intensive applications, dial-up will not be able to keep up. Basic programs start at $5.95 a month. Even though it's dirt cheap, we highly recommend using a high-speed connection for just a few bucks more. It will save you so much time, and free up your phone line for calls!

Website

Some of the concierges we talked to cite their websites as the number-one resource for gaining new clients. Others credit their blog popularity for streaming new customers their way. Still others note that referrals from satisfied clients were number one with websites and blogs as a very close number two. Valerie Fidan uses her blog to keep her male clients connected to global trends, restaurant openings, events, new gadgets, luxury news, and tutorials. Though her educational blog was created as a gift to her clients, it's also an appealing draw to web-surfing men pursuing a luxury lifestyle, and she gets noticed. She doesn't invest in advertising, rather, she puts her

> **Smart Tip** *Tip...*
> Rags-to-riches entrepreneur, author, and motivational speaker Jim Rohn said, "One customer, well taken care of, could be more valuable than $10,000 worth of advertising."

efforts into internet marketing and doing a phenomenal job knowing, "Clients will tell their friends. Word-of-mouth marketing is the best advertisement."

Kathy S., the personal concierge in Elkhart, Indiana, once planned a wedding in Carmel, California. The world is truly getting smaller!

Designing Your Website

Some concierges create their own websites and others hire designers. Ultimately, the choice is up to you. You have to look at your own computer skills, budget, and the type of image you're looking to portray and decide what works. The concierges who hired site designers to build their sites were all happy with their decision. All they had to do was supply the information they wanted to include in their sites. Sites can be very simple, just one page giving the company's name, address, and phone number; or they can include multiple pages with photos and even music, as well as basic business information. It's wise to do your research on this one and get recommendations from your friends or other business owners who have had their websites designed. Also, look at sites to see what features you like and don't like. If you see a site you really like, look at the bottom of the page, it will usually have the name of the designer and contact information.

Costs of having a website built for you vary widely depending on what type of site you want, how in demand the designer is, and what type of experience he or she has. Calling a few places at random, we found that costs could be anywhere from $199 to several thousand dollars. We talked to one web designer who said a client had paid him $12,000 to design a site with multiple pages, tons of photos, and music on each page. Although it cost a pretty penny, the site was a beauty, the designer said. Keep in mind that you can start on the low end, with a website offering just your basic business information, and add the bells and whistles later. The free, self-design sites can be useful if you have a little patience and can put some time into gathering great photos, sorting through templates, and writing copy. Check out www.weebly.com for easy to use tools like drag and drop for image, video, and copy placement, and over 70 professional design templates. Weebly has free hosting, too.

Hosting Your Website

You can have all the content created for your website, but you have to actually put it up on the internet before anyone can see it. You can find a slew of companies that host your non-business personal web page for free. But since you are running a business, you will likely have to pay to have your site hosted. Yahoo! Small Business and www.godaddy.com, are geared perfectly for small business users to quickly and affordably register their website address, host their website, create the pages, and even manage online marketing campaigns with a one-stop shop. Prices start at around $5 a month (or lower if you buy a year at a time) for the most basic services.

Getting Your Name Out

Every concierge we interviewed emphasized the importance of having business stationery because it creates the professional image you want your clients to have of you and your new business. What exactly do you need when it comes to stationery? For starters, you should have business cards, letterhead, and envelopes.

Since this is one of the few real expenses you'll incur, you really shouldn't cut corners here. But, you can shop around. Look at your local print shop and online resources as well. A competitively priced internet option is www.gotprint.com. In addition, www.overnightprints.com promises a 24-hour turnaround on most jobs.

Startup Advertising

We will discuss advertising more in Chapter 6, but we want to give you an idea of how much some concierges spent on advertising when they launched their businesses. One concierge designed and wrote all the copy for her brochure and incurred only the cost of printing and mailing, a sum of about $250.

Another concierge bought newspaper ads, had fliers made up, and also mailed some materials to potential clients. She spent approximately $1,000 on her initial ad campaign. Another concierge advertised mostly by word of mouth and tacking self-designed fliers on bulletin boards around town. She estimates she spent about $50 on her complete campaign.

You can decide what's right for you and how much money you can afford to spend. But if you have no clients at all, a large ad campaign might be a wise place to start.

Getting Coverage

Since the first edition of this book came out, insurance companies have begun to acknowledge the concierge industry and work toward developing a proper category for it. There are different insurance packages available that address the different aspects of concierge services, but many concierges complain that their maximum coverage isn't high enough for the potential lawsuits they might incur. Check out some of these carriers and their industry specific offerings: www.norman-spencer. com, www.benefitresourcing.net, www.amfam.com, and www.petsitllc.com. For help on making an insurance choice appropriate to your service offerings, read EK Errands Express's great article on it: www.ek-errands-express.com/Errand-Concierge_Startup_Info.html.

Most experts agree that you should choose an amount of coverage as least as great as the amount that someone could sue you for. And try going through an independent insurance agent that sells policies from many different companies. She may know of just the answer for getting you coverage in your area.

Several insurance representatives told us that, unless you have employees, you shouldn't need any special coverage. If you do have employees, you'll want to check into workers' compensation coverage, which can cost around $500 to $3,000 per year but can vary widely depending on where you live. If you're transporting people

Equipment Checklist

You can use this checklist as a guide for equipping your office. This list is not carved in stone, and it may contain more (or fewer) items than you need for your office. Look it over, add to it, and make changes as needed.

❑ Computer $ _____

❑ USB flash drive   _____

❑ Printer/scanner combination   _____

❑ Office productivity software   _____

❑ Accounting software   _____

❑ Contact management software   _____

❑ Phone system (two or three lines)   _____

❑ Voice mail or answering machine   _____

❑ PDA   _____

❑ Cellular phone   _____

❑ Surge protector   _____

❑ Calculator   _____

❑ Extra printer cartridge   _____

❑ Internet modem   _____

❑ Printer/copier/fax paper   _____

❑ Letterhead stationery/business cards   _____

❑ Miscellaneous office supplies   _____

during the course of your business, the cost could go up substantially. You'll also want to make sure your employees are fully insured if they are going to be driving for your company. And every concierge we talked to who had employees purchased Employee Dishonesty Bonds. These bonds protect you, the business owner, from liability in the event your employees commit dishonest acts while performing their duties.

Most concierges said it is important to at least have general liability insurance, although they all reported some confusion when their insurance company attempted to categorize their business. According to the personal concierges we interviewed, there is no specific "concierge" category within insurance companies. Some concierges have even found their insurance carriers were classifying them under "limousine companies" because there was no specific category for them. As the concierge business continues to grow, expect to see the industry get its own category. In the meantime, you can still get liability insurance as a business owner.

Legal and Accounting Services

As we've mentioned, it's always wise to consult an attorney if you have legal questions pertaining to your business. If you are going to set up a partnership or corporation, you will definitely need an attorney because certain legal documents have to be filed, and you'll need an attorney's expertise for that. This is another area in which expenses can vary widely depending on what area of the country you live in as well as how much of the attorney's time you take up. Most attorneys charge by the hour; although some offer free consultations, others charge $100 or more for an hour-long consultation. Call around and also ask friends or other business owners to refer you to a good lawyer.

Don't be afraid to barter your services for legal and financial advice. Jennifer C. of Gainesville, Georgia, got to know an attorney through her chamber of commerce. She told him about her business, and after talking a bit, she asked him to review some of her contracts. He agreed to look at them and give his advice in exchange for her picking up his dry cleaning for an agreed-upon period. He loved the service so much that she kept him as a client even after the legal work was completed.

> **Smart Tip**
> Did you know that the IRS has all sorts of business publications available for the business owner? And they're free! Check out its website at www.irs.gov or give it a call at (800) TAX-FORM.

Some personal concierges have used legal services, like Pre-paid Legal Services (www.prepaidlegal.com), paying a small set amount each month to have unlimited contact with an attorney via the telephone during regular business hours. They can also review documents and contracts for you, send letters to help settle disputes, and even represent you at trial, all for a flat fee.

Is It Raining Money?

Even though getting a personal concierge service up and running costs relatively little, it still takes a bit of money, especially if you don't already have a good computer, cell phone, and other necessary equipment. So, where should the money come from? Some personal concierges use their savings; others take out loans; and still others borrow from family or friends. And there are also many other avenues.

Jennifer C. used money she received in a settlement after an automobile accident to start her business. Another concierge shared, "I originally looked into a small business loan but after realizing that the majority of banks wanted you to be in business for three years, or have a substantial amount of equity or assets to use as collateral, I decided not to apply. I had some money left over from refinancing my house and that is what I used."

Since the amount of money required to get a concierge business up and running is relatively small, most concierges said if you are short on capital the best way to get funds is to look for a loan from family members or friends. Generally, unless you need a considerable amount of capital, you shouldn't need to seek out a traditional loan.

Getting Help

As the number of personal concierge businesses grows, companies are emerging that will, for a fee, set up entrepreneurs in their own personal concierge businesses. It's a bit different from franchising in that most companies charge only a one-time fee, and after getting new concierges on their feet, leave them on their own. Go to your favorite search engine and type in "Start a personal concierge business" and look at all the pretty links.

Triangle Concierge offers consulting services dealing with everything from sample contracts for concierges to a business plan. Its site also offers a concierge bookstore, where potential concierges can get info on vendors, meeting and event planning, and much more. Angel At Your Service offers many different products for running your concierge business. It's also developing a traveling seminar, called Errand and Concierge Service University (www.ecsuniversitytraining.com) to teach the industry basics. You'll find details in the Appendix on how to contact all of the concierges we interviewed for this book. But do your own research, too. Kellye G.

found the perfect answer for her training needs, "I contacted a concierge doing business in Austin and asked to pay her a consulting fee to help me. I drove to Austin to meet her."

Concierge consultants have certainly found a niche. Some reportedly charge between $800 to $2,000 per person for a three-day seminar on the basics of getting a personal concierge company up and running. Put your calculator to those numbers and it doesn't take long to figure out why someone created that niche.

So What Do You Do?
Daily Operations

Now we're going to tackle the daily ins and outs of running a personal concierge business, and although that might sound very buttoned-up and serious, this will be a fun chapter. You'll hear about a typical day in the life of a concierge and some of the requests—both the exotic and mundane—that personal concierges have received. You will find out how concierges handle billing and also learn some valuable customer service tips.

Putting in the Hours

One of the best things about the life of an entrepreneur is that you set your own schedule. If you're not a morning person and you don't have to see clients first thing in the morning, then you don't even have to set an alarm. But come 2 p.m., you might find yourself working like a maniac, especially if you're the type of person who hits your high-energy peak in the afternoon. The point is, you can decide what kind of hours you want to work and how you want to structure your work hours, as long as you can meet your clients' needs.

Keep in mind, if you do work odd hours from a home office, your clients don't ever have to know your work habits or even that you work from home. With today's technology, you'll likely be communicating via email, voice mail, or fax. If there is a need for a face-to-face meeting with a client, you can always set up a business lunch.

Lindsey Doolittle of At Your Service (www.lindseysevents.com) in Minneapolis, Minnesota, makes her schedule revolve around her daughter. Right now she is taking on less work, working part time for a couple more years so she can spend quality mommy time. She does her creative brainstorming once the baby is in bed. and taught her to say "Sh-h-h! Baby working!" Lindsey is able to balance parenting time with high quality service by limiting her client list.

A Day in the Life

Wondering what a regular workday might be like once you get your business off the ground? Of course, "regular" means different things to different people. Many variables may affect your day, such as whether you have a home office or an office away from home, whether you work full time or part time, and whether you serve mostly corporate clients or mostly personal clients.

Loreine G. says she typically wakes up "around 6 A.M. to work out, shower, and dress. I hit the computer and make the errand schedule for the day, which an employee will take at 9 A.M. I usually man the computer until 7 P.M. when there is typically some event to go to, and then I come home and continue to work until around 10 P.M."

Abbie Martin, a concierge in Australia, describes her day like a to-do list, "Work for a client in their office on administration and marketing tasks. Visit clients' homes to water garden or let in cleaner/tradesperson. Order gift/flowers on behalf of clients.

Grocery shopping for clients. Phone calls to coordinate trades people/new suppliers for my clients." A busy girl indeed!

Kathy S. looks at her week to describe the regular schedule of her business, "During the week I make several visits to people's homes for pet sitting duties. Generally, I have one weekly shopping trip for clients. I try to group my requests together to save on trips. I make at least one trip to the mall or specialty store. I spend the rest of the time answering questions, doing marketing, returning emails, and

attending networking events. I also find time to do longer term projects like research invitations for a wedding I'm planning." The day we spoke with her she also packed in an appearance on a local radio show and a luncheon talk geared toward making Valentine's Day special at her local Elks Club.

Larissa E. echoes the sentiments of most of the concierges we interviewed, "That's the great part—no two days are the same. Some days are really busy from start to finish, and others are pretty slow. Some days I feel like I'm on the phone or computer all day and others I'm busy running around like a chicken with its head cut off." The one thing they know they will be doing every day is juggling many tasks, and they must be prepared to do that. Some of them carry smartphones, PDAs, or other similar task-management gadgets while they are on the go. Others use filing systems or databases in the office.

When asked how many projects they might take on in an average day, some of the personal concierges said there were too many to count; others, who had smaller operations, said their best guess would be dozens. Concierges say it's difficult to estimate how many tasks they perform because some of their duties are so routine, such as calling clients or vendors, checking email, etc. But make no mistake; most concierges are high-energy, incredibly busy people who virtually never sit still during their workday.

Concierges also say no two clients are the same. Some clients call and want something done yesterday; others generally give the concierge some notice. But as a rule, most concierges say they receive lots of last-minute requests. "It can definitely throw a wrench in things if you're going in one direction and have to change your pace," Cynthia says. "But it's also par for the course, and it's one of the things I enjoy about my work—the unknown."

Making Fantasies Come True

Silvia Oppenheim remembers a touching card she received from a husband who said she saved his marriage. He and his wife were stumped on how to prepare his mother's home for her return from the hospital following a major surgery. They lived over an hour away, both had full-time jobs, and the renovation had to include handicapped features that required major construction. Silvia set to work researching ramps, cleaning air ducts for clean living comfort, creating an art room for stimulating projects, and even stocking the home with fresh flowers and home cooked treats. The

Sure, as Long as It's Legal

We asked concierges all over the United States to give us some of the most unusual requests they had received from clients. In most of these cases, the concierge was able to come through for the client.

○ Arrange a wedding ceremony on the front steps of a nationally known museum located in Cleveland with only three days notice.

○ Move a playhouse from one backyard to another.

○ Pick up a pet dog from the pound after he had escaped.

○ Physically wake up a hung-over employee, get them showered, and to work.

○ Complete a purse exchange. Two sets of grandparents were visiting their kids during a holiday and the respective grannies left for home with the other's purse. The concierge had to do a purse exchange at 11 P.M. on a Sunday night because one set of grandparents was flying out the next morning.

○ Catch two cats who may or may not bring dead things along with them. One concierge had a client that had already relocated to another home in another town, but had left behind part of her stuff and her two cats. The concierge took care of the cats on a regular basis, but on this particular day the cleaning woman had been in and the cats ran out. Her client begged

Sure, as Long as It's Legal, continued

her to go to the house and make sure the cats made their way back inside, and clean up any dead animals they may have hunted and killed during their escape. Fortunately, no animals were harmed in the story.

○ Deliver a tube of toothpaste, 35 miles away. One concierge works for several dental offices. One office was out of a specialty, prescription toothpaste, but located one at another office. The concierge made a 70-mile-roundtrip to pick up and deliver the toothpaste as a patient waited in the office.

○ A list of every Pizza Hut and In-N-Out Burgers between Los Angeles and Coronado, California. A member of the Saudi Arabian royal family wanted one concierge to find out.

○ A used golf-green mower. The client wanted to turn his backyard into a putting green. This one took some time, the concierge said.

○ A favorite laundry detergent from Puerto Rico. A client on the East Coast wanted to have it shipped over.

○ A rare, authentic 1882 Standard Oil Co. stock certificate signed by John D. Rockefeller. As long as a client has the money to back up the request, almost anything may be obtained. And this item was.

○ A place where the Moscow Circus could bathe a bear. A concierge located an outdoor fountain and got permission for the bear to take a bath.

○ The University of Alabama Marching Band. A client requested this for a husband's birthday.

○ A personal chef to fly to Greece. One client needed a chef to come and cook for the duration of a family vacation. No problem.

○ Diet Hawaiian Punch. A client was disappointed when he learned his favorite diet Hawaiian Punch was being discontinued, so he asked his concierge to call all over the United States and buy up supplies of the punch. She was able to find enough punch to last him for a couple of months, which turned out to be perfect because the punch only had a shelf life of about three months. After that? Guess he had to find a new flavor of punch.

○ Spending $500 (of the client's money) and 12 hours to deliver a specialty birthday cake to a very lucky little girl. A client in Florida wanted her daughter to receive a cake from her favorite bakery in Chicago, and when all was said and done that little old birthday cake cost 12 hours and $500 dollars.

elderly woman beamed upon coming home to such a welcoming sanctuary, and Silvia was thanked profusely for coming to the rescue. She remarked at how many seniors just need someone to shop and cook for them, and many times she's hired by the children of those seniors who can't accommodate all of those tasks and still have time to themselves.

Kevin of The Daily Plan It told us that after writing a handwritten thank-you card to a client he noticed that the client kept the card displayed with other sentimental items in his home. Never underestimate the warm reverberations of a nicely worded note that's actual rather than virtual.

Valerie Fidan keeps track of and acknowledges her clients' preferences, tastes, favorite sports teams, birthdays, and milestones.

Cynthia tells of a client whose daughter wanted to see pop superstar Ricky Martin in concert. The only problem was that the concert had been sold out for weeks. But the client knew who to call—his personal concierge. "We were able to get tickets for his daughter to go to the concert, and his daughter was so happy that I can't even begin to tell you. So was the client," Cynthia says, laughing. "He's pretty popular around his house these days."

She has other stories, including some about a client who wanted 18-karat-gold fixtures and a custom-made bidet installed in her bathroom. "I'm serious," Cynthia says. "Could I make this up?" She's able to recall these incidents because she keeps a book detailing the most memorable requests she's received from clients.

Although there are humorous moments, Cynthia takes her job very seriously. "There is a definite trust factor that must be there between the client and the concierge," she says. "For instance, I had one client who recently made a $200,000 purchase based simply on my recommendation. My clients trust and respect my instincts, and I take the responsibility very seriously."

But don't think that every request gets filled. Even concierges, as much as they hate to, sometimes have to tell the client they just can't do it. "A few years ago, I had a client who called me the day before Bastille Day," says Cynthia. "He wanted me to make a reservation for him at a restaurant in the Eiffel Tower. But there was just no way it was going to happen. I tried, though. I had colleagues in France who just laughed when I called. If my client had just called me sooner, it could have worked out, but they were so booked up that it was impossible."

As we mentioned earlier, the concierges interviewed for this book were gracious and extremely willing to share their experiences. But there were some areas where they weren't willing to offer specifics. None of them wanted to give away their secrets on how they can fulfill last-minute requests or snag impossible-to-get concert tickets. One personal concierge, while claiming she wasn't worried about competition, coyly said that if she divulged her tips, every personal concierge would have the chance to elbow in on her business.

All the concierges interviewed agreed that they have sources and contacts in every area imaginable. How did they get those sources and contacts? Some of them made contacts when they worked as hotel concierges. Others networked with people in various businesses and gradually developed contacts that way. Although the concierges took separate paths, all of them played up the networking factor as a central component of their ongoing success. Many of them consider fellow concierges friends, but the competition factor still exists. They don't divulge every tidbit of information about their business when they lunch with a fellow concierge or run into them at a business function.

Filling the Bills

You might be wondering how your clients will be billed or what to charge for your time and effort. You want your clients to be satisfied, of course, but you also want to have a nice annual income from your business. You would probably like to get a tried-and-true fee schedule that you can use. But in the rapidly developing personal concierge industry, how you charge your clients is another one of those gray areas with no set-in-stone guidelines. What and how you are paid for your efforts is another area that you will have to research and design along the lines of your own preferences and ideas.

Most concierges have developed their own system of pricing their services, and they guard it like it's Fort Knox. Since they worked so hard to set up their business without a blueprint, you can bet they aren't going to give away those hard-earned secrets. But there are a few general patterns.

Sign on the Dotted Line

After you land each new client, there is one very important step you must take—draw up a contract. The contract spells out exactly what type of service you provide. It also covers fees, how often the client is billed, and when payment is due (usually in 30 days). The contract should also discuss who has the right to terminate the contract, how much notice is required, and any other particulars. It's always wise to have an attorney give the contract a once-over before finalizing it. The attorney may spot some red flags you didn't see. Don't think you can skip dealing with contracts. Every personal concierge we interviewed said contracts are vital. They protect you—and your clients.

Most concierges charge their clients membership fees. Some memberships allow a certain number of requests each month for one annual fee. For those types of memberships, annual fees might start at around $1,000 to $1,500. Other memberships might be available for a smaller annual fee. For instance, if a client wants to use the concierge services only once or twice a year for small errands, a fee of $500 might be set up. Fees and contracts vary among concierges and clients.

Corporate clients are charged much higher fees because they require more services per month. For corporations, membership fees vary widely depending on the size of the

Smart Tip

Come up with a standard reply that you can use in response to client requests. Although some hotel concierges use the very formal "That would be my pleasure," or "My pleasure," a personal concierge might want to come up with something a bit less formal. Tailor your reply phrase to the types of clients you'll be working with. Be creative and remember that a casual response style might work for some clients but not others.

company and how many requests each employee is allowed. Again, most concierges would not divulge exact fees, but a ballpark annual fee for a corporate client with many employees who are each allowed multiple requests each month could start at $5,000. More employees and a greater number of requests could drive the fee much higher.

It might be possible for a concierge who is just starting out to forgo annual membership fees and charge clients per request or per hour. For instance, you could agree to do some shopping for a client for $25 to $75 per hour or charge him a onetime fee that you settle on before you start. But most of the concierges we talked to prefer to charge membership fees because that way they are assured steady business (and a steadier income). Most of them prefer to fill six to eight requests from member clients each month rather than tackle one chore for someone who calls out of the blue and may never call again.

What happens to the bill when you've tried your best but are unable to meet the client's need? While every personal concierge has his or her own way of doing business, the norm seems to be that the client will not be charged the full amount. If considerable time and effort go into trying to fulfill a request, adding a partial fee may be appropriate.

Bright Idea

Call your clients at least once a week. Sometimes, just that simple phone call will jog their memory and remind them they do need your assistance after all!

It may sound a bit complicated at first, but after you decide what types of services you want to offer and what types of fees to charge for each, you can get your system up and running in no time. While there is no blueprint for this part of the concierge business, we've given you some ideas about how to structure your fees. As many personal concierges mentioned, when they started in this very new industry, nothing was in place to tell them how to charge their clients. They developed their own systems, and they came out on top. So will you!

Lots of Pencil Pushing

Let's change gears and talk about daily operations like paperwork and pencil pushing. You didn't think your new career was going to be all fun and games, did you? Yes, there are going to be times when you will have to turn your attention to paperwork. Things like operating expenses, for instance. I know, your eyes are probably already glazing over. But you'll have to pay close attention to such details if you want your new business to succeed, and if you want those checks from clients to keep rolling in. Do I have your attention?

For starters, you'll have daily, weekly, and monthly monetary concerns in your new business, as well as typical operating expenses. Keeping track of your expenses includes itemizing home office expenses, mileage (personal concierges do typically pay for their own mileage), and monies spent on goods for various clients. Sometimes a personal concierge will carry around a wish list for an established client. Concierges who have longstanding working relationships with clients might pick up items, knowing that they will be reimbursed.

Depending on what types of services a concierge provides, other expenses may include fees for car rentals, clothing, concert tickets, airline or trip expenses, and so on.

Smart Tip

Set aside a certain time of the month to devote to paperwork so it doesn't pile up. There are lots of software programs that make it easier to keep up with facts and figures. You can store files on your computer and have information at your fingertips. If you feel more secure having a file cabinet, you can go that route. Try buying brightly colored folders so it won't seem like such drudgery.

You will have another important bookkeeping chore if you structure your business based on membership fees. That chore will be to keep track of how many requests you have filled for a client each month. Most concierges said that, after a while, they develop a certain relationship and trust with their clients and will sometimes allow them more requests than spelled out in their contract. The client will certainly remember that sort of good-faith favor when it's time to sign a new contract.

The concierges said if a client's requests go way overboard one month, they will usually send an invoice the following month noting the extra services and requesting

High Standards

Although Les Clefs d'Or is for hotel concierges, many personal concierges have adopted some of the organization's standards. The following practices are specific customer-service standards members of Les Clefs d'Or are expected to follow:

○ Listen to guests with an attentive ear.

○ Return all calls in a timely manner.

○ Always thank the guest if he or she remembers you in some way. Send thank-you notes whenever possible.

○ Never call guests by their first names.

○ Always maintain professional relationships with guests.

○ Never double-book restaurants for guests.

○ Tactfully decline illegal or unethical requests from guests.

○ Never promise guests anything unless you are sure you can deliver.

○ Always provide guests with written confirmations of their requests.

○ Advise guests upfront of surcharges or service fees on tickets or other requests.

○ Always tell guests if their seats at an event will be partially obstructed or in a poor location.

○ Inform guests of dress codes at restaurants.

○ Learn to evaluate guests by their manner, dress, and preferences. Remember that what might be good for one guest may be unsuitable for another.

payment. Most said they balance their books and do their accounting activities once a month.

Pleasing the Client

In every interview for this book, two words kept popping up over and over again: customer service. How important is customer service in the personal concierge industry? Well, those two words pretty much embody what the profession is all about.

"To succeed in this business, you have to have a total customer service attitude. The customer is always right. You have to work to always make it better. So many people [just starting out] think this is just a quick way to earn a few bucks, but it's absolutely a business. You have to have passion to succeed at your own business," says Kathy S. "And," she adds, "communication is key." Abbie agrees that strong communication is important, adding "flexibility and a willingness to get the job done no matter what" top the list.

Loreine G. suggests a few softer qualities for the successful concierges, "empathy, adaptability, persistence, and good ethics." Other traits noted by most of the concierges include being well-organized and an excellent time-manager.

Kathy S. describes the scope of her services by telling prospective clients, "My services are only limited by your imagination and the laws of the state of Indiana." Many concierges mention that they also make sure to point out the legalities involved. So, we wondered, what kinds of illegal activities were these hardworking entrepreneurs approached with?

Two types of requests occurred regularly. In some cases, people thought the term "personal concierge" was some sort of code for an escort service. In other cases, people want a concierge to make a liquor store run for them. While the first would strike most people living outside Nevada as illegal, the second may cause you to pause. In most states, people can only purchase and transport alcohol for their own private use. Even if your client is of legal drinking age, it's likely that you cannot purchase and deliver alcohol to him. Check your local laws to make sure you're sticking to the letter of the law.

Outstanding Customer Service
Your Primary Focus

What can I do for you? This is how one concierge answers her phone at both home and work. She also repeats that sentiment at the end of each conversation before hanging up. It may seem like a simple thing, but it is the style of thinking that will lead you to a great customer service model. You have to feel it

▲

and mean it and on those days you don't feel it first, be ready to fake it until you make it, as the old saying goes.

Your Happiness Is Theirs

Loving to serve others is not always an inborn trait, rather, it can be cultured by experiencing the feeling of giving and forming an addiction to it. Have you ever known someone who was always thinking of you or just made you feel good about yourself? You craved that person's attention, didn't you? You may have even come to rely on them for your day-to-day fix of happy. Those people we love are so warm and wonderful to be around because they are addicted to the cycle of giving. We beam our gratitude at them and they want to give more. They become prone to acting on generous thoughts and the results are like a drug.

To be the cause of happiness, relief, relaxation, and even emotional and mental health is powerful. Often, the afterglow of giving without ulterior motvie is the only reward givers get. All businesses have to offer a thoughtful level of customer service

> **Bright Idea**
> "Here is a simple but powerful rule—always give people more than what they expect to get".
> —Nelson Boswell

to thrive, but the person addicted to giving does it without reward because they believe generosity and goodness are what makes the world (or their business world) go around.

Practice, Practice

If you aren't quite there yet, don't despair. Inroads can be made by practicing. When you see how much people appreciate your warm gestures, you'll want to do

Plant the Seeds: Watch Your Garden Grow

Here are some things you can do to stand out and practice building a standard of customer service that people will tell their friends about:

○ Send one short, helpful email to every person you know. If you're are asking yourself if you should really put that much time into this, remember that

Plant the Seeds, continued

every person you know, with the exception of your crazy uncle who doesn't own a telephone and shoots rats down by the river, is a possible networking connection and customer. Your personalized email should say something like this: "This made me think of you. Is there any way I can help make your life easier? I'm trying to get a feel for how I can be the most helpful form of relief as a concierge."

O In correspondence with customers (like billing emails) and people you're trying to build relationships with, include a link to an article related to each person's efforts in life. Don't just send out an email about cute puppies. It has to something helpful. If you need ideas, think information, health tips, nutritional information, business help, safety techniques, cutting-edge, specialized gear or tools, or networking connections.

O Buy inexpensive, useful things for people occasionally, just because you know they'd find them of use. We can learn from one woman's experience receiving a special gift. Amy S. had a fall from a ladder, breaking her hip, at her construction job. The previous year she had been feeling that perhaps she wasn't tough enough to work in a male dominated field and had been getting some sexist remarks in the elevator and break room. As she recovered in her hospital room she received a small package with a card attached. It was from all of her male coworkers, who had written, "You are one tough broad and we miss you. Get better soon!" The gift was a pink hammer patterned with tiny white flowers. She was so touched because the gift and card, while hard won, showed they thought about her and cared about the struggles that were unique to her life. Choose offerings that show you've been paying attention. That hammer sits in a curio case in Amy's living room.

O Buy a dozen yellow, cheery roses once every two weeks and divide them up between your customers. On your visits for household tasks, leave two or three roses in vases in each client's home. Silvia Oppenheim gets emotional responses from her use of flowers to cheer people up. She also leaves chocolates on their pillows to acknowledge anniversaries and sometimes leaves fresh baked bread for them, just because.

O Have a treasure chest of freebies to give away if you fail to deliver on a promise. While it's obvious that you should never promise what you can't

Plant the Seeds, continued

deliver, mistakes do happen and as you mature in your business, you'll understand more clearly what your limitations are and be less likely to get yourself into this situation. When a mistake is made or your service just isn't quite what you would have liked to give to your client, acknowledge it before they do, sincerely apologizing. Then offer a gift certificate for a hand massage, inexpensive lunch somewhere unique, or a free hour of errand running.

O Use the opening of a new restaurant or club in your area as a chance to mingle socially with your clients and introduce them to one another, calling it a party without all the work. Announcing the latest hotspot in town and their All You Can Eat Sushi Bar Wednesdays, or signaling a two-for-one children's haircut special at a fun hair concept salon will show you've got your ear to the ground for their needs. Once you position yourself as a local authority on what's fresh and worth experiencing in your area, people will begin asking your opinion about all kinds of services, and this is an opportunity to sell more of your time and detailed offerings.

more. You'll then start attracting new attention, respect, loyalty, and generous gestures from others. One of the key facets to not burning out on giving is to budget your time, understand how much energy you can spare, not deplete your reserves, and finally, don't give away your gold to those who will squander it.

Indelible Memories

We asked a wide range of consumers and service providers about what their most memorable customer service experiences were and without a doubt, the thing they all had in common was going above and beyond. Remember why these above and beyond examples of customer service stayed in the minds of our survey participants for years as you set your own standards. Here's what was special to them:

- Shortly after the September 11th tragedies, a traveler en route home from Madrid, left a special souvenir doll in a New York City airport restaurant. Much dismayed to find the doll missing when she got home, she called Northwest

Airlines, who conducted a search of the entire airport, found the doll, and sent it to her, free of charge.

- A vacationer recalls his first day arriving at a corporate-owned, private lodge with a group of guests. The entire staff at the lodge knew everyone's name in the group almost immediately, without nametags!

- An installer from Direct TV came to a home in northern Michigan to try and install a satellite system, after six other workers from his company had come and left with no success connecting the system. He spent eight hours there, making numerous phone calls to make it happen, and he did. The family was extremely grateful to be able to finally watch whatever they wanted on TV in their remote home.

- A harried mother reported appreciating the same thing in all of her favorite businesses. When customer service is detailed to the point of being obsessive-compulsive, it helps customers like her because they catch things that she forgets, which is why she sought them out in the first place – because she can't do it all by herself.

Randomize the Love

Unexpected gifts and perks make people feel special. To avoid "training" your customers to expect something extra from you, switch up the types of gifts or perks and reasons for giving them. For example, give a gift certificate for a free manicure as a Happy Spring present, but not one for the bigger winter holidays when gestures can get lost in the shuffle. Send clients who refer you to others a bouquet of flowers once a year to say thank you and you can bet they'll talk about you to their friends some more.

Double Duty

Part of your customer service efforts will fall under the category of research. As you look for new experiences on the internet and out on the streets for your customers keep notes for separating what you'll use for great service ideas, what you'd like to feature on your blog or Facebook page, and what you'll just send personalized notes on. You'll find that reading business magazines such as *Entrepreneur* and *Inc.* will give you so many ideas for great customer service models, you'll hardly be able to keep up.

Imagine it Real

We hope that the examples you've seen in this chapter will just be the beginning for the development of your own, unique brand of caring for your flock of customers. For added inspiration, imagine being interviewed for an article on stellar customer service providers, because you've set such an impressive example. That should get you going!

Selling Service
Advertising and Marketing

For your business to be successful, you will need a lot more than just a good computer, fax machine, extra phone lines, and fancy file cabinets. You'll need clients. If this will be your first service-oriented business, you probably don't have a client base yet. Don't despair! In this chapter, we'll discuss ways to promote your business and attract clients. Once you get your first couple of clients and word spreads about what a great job you're doing, you'll soon have more business than you can handle.

So where do you get those first clients? Well, start off by telling everyone you can possibly think of that you have started your own personal concierge business. Your first clients might be your friends and acquaintances or those of family members, neighbors, and customers or operators of businesses you patronize.

"I just started putting the word out to people that I had previously worked with when I was a hotel concierge," says Cynthia A., the personal concierge from San Diego. "In the beginning, some of my clients were family members; others were friends of family members; and others were people I'd known while working at previous jobs."

Getting the Word Out

Letting the world know your business is up and running will bring clients your way. Start by attending some casual business functions and passing out business cards. For instance, find out when your local chamber of commerce, Rotary Club, or Toastmasters group holds meetings. Often, they hold breakfast meetings that can be good "meet and greet" opportunities. A great place to connect to different social interest groups and clubs is www.meetup.com. In Chapter 9 you'll read more about how to use Meetup. If you have the time, start your own networking group. You can broadcast group meetings on Meetup for a very small fee and hold them at a local restaurant or even line up a seminar room at a college or university and publish a print or email newsletter to keep members informed of meeting times and dates.

Publish a Newsletter

Several concierges we spoke with created quarterly or monthly newsletters that they send to clients. You could send a hard copy via snail mail or choose an email format. It's entirely up to you and ultimately, your clients, of course. Many people have had success with an email newsletter delivered by services like Constant Contact. The price goes up based on how many addresses you send to, rather than how often you send information. For up to 500 addresses it's $15 and the rates go up from there. You can include photos, and seasonal reminders, and advertize new services. They also have reporting tools that let you keep track of how many clients are actually opening the newsletter.

Kathy S. sends her newsletter regularly to media outlets in her area. She always makes the topic timely reminding people to "weed out their old books or donate to charities, whatever works for the moment." She always gets a response. The media keep her in mind when they need a spot to fill or an expert to talk about organizing, time management, or giving the perfect gift.

Preparing Your Elevator Speech

In this relatively new business, it pays to have an "elevator speech" or a 30-second spiel that you can rattle off when someone asks "what does that mean?" after you tell them you're a personal concierge. Jennifer C. gave me hers, "I run errands for people. I can take your dog for a walk, your cat to vet, the car to get the oil change, do your grocery shopping, and pick up dry cleaning. I can run down to Atlanta for you to pick something up or drop it off. If any of these things sound good to you, let me know; I'm here to help."

Larissa E. found an obstacle when starting her new business, "I live in the heart of the Ozarks. Too often people don't understand what a concierge service is or does, so I've found it's easier to tell them I'm a personal assistant and they relate much better." Abbie M. relates to that idea, "I'm a personal assistant for anyone—for anyone who needs more time or needs to finish their 'to do' list."

Traditional Advertising

Purchase ad space on www.yelp.com. Yelp is a local service review site, which you can list your business on for free. It can be quite useful to let your customers know you've got a listing there. If you put forth great service you'll get great reviews. One sticky issue that Yelp users have been complaining about is that not all of your reviews are visible all the time because of a random shuffling process. When you only have five or six customers who all give you great reviews it can be disappointing to see that Yelp may only showcase three of those reviews through its randomization process, which has been much publicized and misunderstood. No worries, though, for Yelp is a great place to be seen if you can just hang in there until your customer review base broadens enough to make you look great on it. Of course, the negative is that if there should be a disgruntled person out there, even if that person is not your customer, he can write a negative review that will decrease your average star rating.

Yelp sends out business advice and one of the tidbits it offers as good practice in general can be used to deal with this kind of problem; respond to each reviewer directly online positively. This is visible to other reviewers. If you utilize wonderful customer service online, it will be seen. For example, if a customer says that he wishes your prices were lower, post your response addressing his issue, first thanking him for taking the time to write his review then talk about an option that may be more affordable. Another great reason to use Yelp is its free events listing section, which can link back to your ad and site for more exposure. If you list an event with the name of your business, any Google search for your business name will turn up that event listing.

Put ads in the paper. A couple of the concierges we talked to had some luck with newspaper ads, and though few people actually drag out the big bulky Yellow Pages these days, consider listing online on www.yellowpages.com, and Google's free business listing (www.google.com/placesforbusiness). Don't forget www.craigslist.org ads—they will get you some exposure and they're free. Kevin Miller tries featuring his Daily Plan It service under different titles, in different sections of Craigslist to see which gets a stronger response.

If you're trying to cut costs, you might not want to spend all your money on expensive advertising. Have fliers made up and get permission to post them on bulletin boards in community centers, doctors' offices, dental clinics, or in the break rooms or cafeterias of large companies. The fliers route is one of the least costly, depending on how much you spend for the printing. Many of the concierges we talked to did all of their marketing online, using no paper, which you can read more about in Chapter 9.

You can also send sales letters to potential clients. We've included a sample sales letter and survey to send with it (see pages 97 and 98, respectively). Some of the concierges we talked to covered all the bases and sent sales letters, posted or mailed fliers, and placed ads in newspapers—while others picked one avenue and stuck with it.

Of course, there is always (gulp!) cold calling. Nobody ever looks forward to cold calling because of the fear of rejection. Admittedly, it's no fun calling ten people in a row who say "No" to your pitch. But if you stick with it, that eleventh call could bring a "Yes" and lots of new business.

You Can Never Be Too Prepared

Nancy Roebke, executive director of Profnet Inc., a company that specializes in teaching business professionals how to generate more revenue for their firms, shared a great networking nugget in *NAPO News*, the monthly newsletter of the National Association of Professional Organizers. "Always have a supply of business cards on you at all times," Roebke says. "I know of a man who met a prospective client while on vacation, swimming in a hotel pool in Hawaii. He landed an account with the firm when he produced a business card (laminated, of course!) from his swimming trunks." Laughing at the image of that unusual networking exchange? That smart cookie is probably laughing all the way to the bank.

There are many other ways you can get the word out. You can send informational packets or brochures about your company to the human resources departments of large corporations in your area or deliver brochures to smaller offices. Most people like to put a face with a name; when sending a brochure or other type of flier to potential clients, think about including your photo somewhere on the mailer.

You might also join a mailing service and send your sales letters and other materials to people on mailing lists. Mailing lists focus on all types of demographics, and you can request any particular one you want to target. Dual-income families and successful businesspeople are two groups that are more likely to need concierge services, so keep this in mind when you're selecting mailing lists.

Smart Tip

Tip...

As you collect business cards at various networking functions, jot down comments regarding the new contact on the back of the card. For instance, if you meet a marketing expert who specializes in an area that may help your business in the future, jot down his or her specialty on the back of the card for future reference. Then put all the cards in a spot where you can easily access them.

"My favorite marketing tip is wear a name tag. It invites people to talk to you. Then you are able to chat up the person and talk, talk, talk about your business. The more you talk about it, the easier it gets too. At first I was fumbling for words, but now it's easy and I don't mind asking them if there is something I could do for them to save them time and let them spend more time with their family," says Jennifer C., a Gainesville, Georgia, errand runner and owner of Warp Speed Errands (www. warpspeederrands.com).

A Catch-All Phrase

When you're thinking of ways to reach new clients, consider coming up with a phrase or a slogan that describes the services you offer. For instance, one concierge company proclaims: "Don't put off till tomorrow what you can delegate today." Another concierge came up with this one: "Let us Run—While you Have Fun," Yet another concierge tells customers: "We do it so you don't have to." Another one went with: "Running Errands for the Running Ragged." Once you've chosen a slogan, stick with it. Use it on all of your advertising materials and maybe even on your stationery.

Spinning a Web

You'll also need to make sure you have a website up and running. Just about every concierge interviewed said this was an invaluable tool in reaching potential clients.

▲

Most saw their client bases increase almost as soon as they launched their websites.

Katharine G. feels her website is vital to her business. "Potential clients can find out what services we offer, where we're located, how to get in touch with us, and what we can do for them," she says. "We get feedback from all over the United States. When it comes to promoting our business, I wouldn't even think of not having a website."

Most of the concierges we talked to have websites, although not all of them had them when they launched their businesses. Without exception, the ones who later added websites said they noticed an increase in business almost immediately. Some swapped links or exchanged banners with other sites, meaning that their web pages were promoted on other sites. But

most of these concierges said they felt the greatest success came by registering their sites with search engines. After all, if nobody knows your site is there, what good is it?

Of course, the type of website that will probably get you the most notice—and the most clients—is one that's professionally designed. But if you're short on funds, why not build your own website? The free design tools offered by many of the hosting companies have a variety of templates you can use to get started building a website today. By doing it yourself, you'll save hundreds of dollars since the only cost you will incur is a small monthly fee for the web hosting service.

Dozens of services offer website space, along with instructions geared to those new to the website arena. You can build a site in as little as 30 minutes and you don't even have to know HTML. Just click on a search engine and type in "website hosting" or "website promotion," and you'll get hundreds of choices.

Several companies say they offer "free" web space; however, this often doesn't apply if you intend to use your website for commercial purposes. Be sure to read the Terms and Conditions posted at these companies' websites. You'll likely need to pay at least $5 to $15 a month in web hosting fees. Even before you get your website set up, you can email your friends, family, and acquaintances and tell them that there is a new concierge in town.

> ## Smart Tip
>
> *Tip...*
>
> One of the first things a new website owner should do is look into search engine optimization, or SEO, in order to make sure your website comes up when users search with words such as "personal concierge" or other key phrases that are important to you. Considering hiring a service such as www.registereverywhere.com to get your webpage seen by your potential clients. As your business grows you can consider sponsoring results with specific search engines for a fee, guaranteeing that your site gets top placement in your customers' browsers.

Sales Letter

Ace Concierge Service
123 Elm St., Mayberry, OH 12345
Phone: (123) 555-4567/Fax: (123) 555-4568

October 1, 20xx

Ms. Tammy Timechallenged
777 Upside Down St.
Mayberry, OH 12345

Dear Ms. Timechallenged:

What would you think if someone told you they would take responsibility for all your business and personal errands each day so that you could have more time for yourself and your family? After all, when someone runs a large corporation like you do, you probably have no time for errands.

Well, there's no need to pinch yourself because we can make this dream a reality for you. My services range from the simple to the exotic. My company, Ace Concierge, was founded to help busy professionals like you.

Let me give you a couple of examples.

○ When was the last time your car was washed? Oh, I know. There just aren't enough hours in the day, right? Well, I can make arrangements to pick up your car while you are at work and have it washed, waxed, or detailed, and back to your office before you call it a day.

○ Or maybe you have been thinking about throwing a small dinner party but just don't have time to attend to the details. No problem! I can take care of everything for you.

I'd like to set up a meeting with you at your convenience to talk more in detail about all of the exciting services my company offers. In the meantime, please fill out the enclosed survey, which will give me a better idea of the types of services you might require.

I look forward to talking to you very soon. Please don't hesitate to call me with any questions. I can be reached at (123) 555-4567.

Sincerely,

Eva Errands

Eva Errands, Ace Concierge

P.S. I'm so interested in doing business with you that I'd like to extend a special offer to you. How does one free month of personal concierge services sound? I thought you'd like that! Once you get used to someone taking care of all your personal and business errands for you, I believe you will never want to go back to the way things were. Talk to you soon!

Survey to Enclose with Sales Letter

How often do you think you might use the services of a personal concierge? (Please circle your answer.)

  a. Every day

  b. Once a week

  c. Once a month

  d. Several times a month

What services most interest you?

  a. Errand-type services

  b. Business-related services

  c. Personal services

  d. A combination of the above

Which of the following statements best describes you?

  a. I never have enough hours in the day to get everything done.

  b. I certainly could use some help with personal errands.

  c. If I had an extra pair of hands just one day a week, I could better manage my business.

  d. All of the above

Extra! Extra!

You might try to pitch a story about your new business to your local newspaper. But keep in mind that large papers get hundreds of pitches a week. So make it good. If your community has a weekly paper, you might start there first, since you won't have quite as much competition as at a larger daily paper. Don't give up if you don't hear back from an editor right away. Give it a couple of weeks and then phone the editor to ask if he or she received your information.

How do you know which advertising methods to use? Well, each person—and business—is different. What works for one person might not work for you. So think about your preferences, the clients you want to attract, and how much you can afford

Let's Do Lunch

While you're thinking about ways to promote your business, remember that you can gain a lot by networking with others in your industry. Some of those benefits include:

- ○ Knowledge or insight about your industry
- ○ Advice about how to solve business problems
- ○ Leads on new business opportunities
- ○ Possible joint ventures
- ○ The chance to learn important new skills
- ○ Brainstorming sessions
- ○ Feedback and constructive criticism

So, how do you meet these new "lunch buddies"? There are many ways to find folks like you. Join business clubs and associations. Attend business expos, trade shows, and Meetups. Participate in online business-related forums, email discussion groups, and chat rooms. Of course, there are lots of other ways to network. But to find them, you'll have to do a little networking of your own!

to spend on advertising. Then choose a method or two or three and get going. Once you find something that works for you, stick with it!

As far as ongoing advertising costs are concerned, some concierges said that after they established a client base, they didn't do much advertising apart from their website. Others reported setting aside several hundred dollars per month for advertising. Experiment and see what works for you.

When it comes to promoting your new business, the list of avenues to pursue is endless. So, what are you waiting for? Hop to it. Clients are waiting.

Keep Them Coming Back for More

When you've implemented some of the advertising methods discussed, the clients should start rolling in—and that's a great feeling. But you can't stop there. Now for the hard work: keeping your clients happy so they'll remain your clients for the long haul.

Cynthia A., the San Diego personal concierge, says it is important to touch base with her clients on a regular basis, even if she knows they don't require her services that particular week. "I stay in touch with my clients quite frequently," she says. "At least weekly, and sometimes more often. I have great clients. Sometimes, they will end up calling me first. And they won't have any reason for calling; they just want to touch base. And oftentimes, just in talking, we'll find that they actually do need me to do something for them that week."

Cynthia says she has clients who would prefer that they were her only clients. "And I treat them like they are," she says. "In the beginning, I had one client who was excellent, but I think he really wanted to be my one and only client. Finally, he began to give others referrals about my service, but I think he wishes he could have remained my only client."

It's important for personal concierges to follow a few very important rules when dealing with clients:

- Always return phone calls promptly.
- Try to resolve any problem as soon as possible.
- If the client has a question, try to answer it quickly.

We've said it several times throughout this book but we really can't overemphasize this point: Customer service is crucial. Without good customer service, you won't have any clients. Don't make it hard for your clients to get in touch with you—it might cost you future business. Make sure they can reach you or leave a message by phone or voice mail, fax, or email.

Social Media Does It All

If you've ever read a blog or product review, watched a video on YouTube, or surfed Facebook, you've indulged in social media, and its methods have influenced you. Every time you step off the diving board into that pool of endless, connected resources on the internet, you are making yourself available to be influenced, marketed to, and ultimately sold on an idea or product. One minute you can be looking at your friend's vacation photos on Facebook and the next thing you know, you're reading some guys' blog about how to pack light for a backpacking trip through Ireland, all because your friends posted that link near their photos. That same "speed of light" interconnected magic can increase your business presence.

Knowing that knowledge is exchanged easily, rapidly, and frequently without cost online, today's forward thinking entrepreneurs recognize this valuable resource as the ticket to all they need, sometimes without spending one advertising dollar. If you're a novice to social media, don't worry. In this chapter, we'll give you assignments and examples of how our panel of concierges uses it to their advantage.

The Major Venues

Without getting too much into each social media website and its stats, we can tell you that there are a few main players that most everyone seems to be using, and that you should, too. It's best to showcase yourself on sites with large audiences, while refining your focus once you're on there so you don't get lost in the shuffle.

Abide by the Laws for Success

- Dedicate at least 45 minutes a day to using your social networks to connect to your audience and give them useful information. This is law in the world of making social media work for your business. Update your blog and Facebook page, answer emails, and send out Tweets. Once in a while post a new, useful video on YouTube and send a notice through the above listed venues that you've done so.

- Be as courteous as you would in a job interview, putting your best face forward.

- Keep it refined. Use correct punctuation and writing skills and don't give in to the current style of slovenly writing habits and abbreviations. You'll stand out from the crowd when you choose to respect the written word and ultimately, the people who are reading yours.

- Never use foul language or post unprofessional material, including photos that in any way do not look professional.

- Try and answer every person who writes you, even if it's brief.

- Keep correspondence timely. Don't make the fan base you'll eventually build wait days for a response from you.

- Post fresh material every few days, even if it's just a photo with a link to another site.

- Don't overuse your audience's attention span. If you contact them too often or ask them for too much, you'll lose them. People are busy. Once a week is about right for short notices and monthly for detailed announcements.

- Don't ask for anything. People are busy and don't want more things in their lives that require their energy. By simply giving, your business will invite inquiry.

Get Started!

Create a Meetup profile on www.meetup.com in three groups that align with your niche. If you offer household services, find the single mother or father groups. If you offer alternative health services and resources, join groups whose key interests involve health. You get the picture.

Go to the Meetup meetings and socialize. Tell people what you're doing and ask if you can help them in any way. Bring your cards and hand them out at the end conversations. If someone gives you her card follow up immediately with a short, pleasant note thanking her for good conversation. Always have the link to your website at the bottom of your email.

Facebook is another way to hobnob with people, post advertisements, and keep in touch with your "friends." Build a profile on www.facebook.com and use the tips listed above when corresponding. Go to events that relate to your industry and post photos you've taken at the events. Then send out messages for people to check out the photos. Take advantage of the fact that people love to look at photos of themselves and you'll have a bunch of people looking at your Facebook page. Post helpful, pertinent tips that they'll be interested in with links to your blog, website, and YouTube pages. Don't worry, we'll get to all that in a minute.

With its limited character allowance, www.twitter.com is great for short alerts and posting links to longer news sources. People use it for anything from offering immediate, time-sensitive specials for their businesses to just telling jokes and staying connected. As you drive through town and see new businesses opening up, why not "tweet" your customers? They might like these news flashes. Ask them first if they'd like to subscribe to your Twitter account before starting your news frenzy.

YouTube is a great place to post short videos about anything in your field. They can be tutorials, entertainment, or anything that is helpful to your audience. Think gift giving. Take that opportunity to post the links again of your site and blog. Get a cheap digital camera with video capability online or at Best Buy and start making videos and posting them. Your camera should come with the appropriate cords and download software.

Create a blog on www.wordpress.com or any free site you like better. Do a search for "free blog." Because there are so many out there it is just a matter of which style and functions you prefer. The important thing is to start writing and don't stop! Topics like what's fun to do in your city and unique products and services you believe in are a good place to start. Fifteen minutes each day about topics relevant to your crowd is the minimum you should commit to and again, post your other social media links next to your fascinating articles so your fans can explore you further.

Take It from the Pros

Each of our concierge consultants uses social media in a different, creative way. It's interesting to see how each of them has customized the internet as a tool for their own unique goals.

Silvia Oppenheim uses Facebook in many ways but one thing she does that people tune in for is posting recipes of the delights she gives customers. Imagine that Silvia has graciously left you a delicious Passover tartlet after delivering your dry cleaning, because she remembered that you're Jewish and don't have time to bake. As you savor the scrumptious dessert you tune into Silvia's Facebook page, knowing she'll post the recipe. Once you're there, you find out about all the other services she offers.

Jennifer Knoch of Radar Concierge (www.radar-msp.com) doesn't really need a website. Her blog serves her needs just as well. She keeps her blog entries local, posting travel itineraries, gift referrals, local restaurants, and shopping recommendations. Her gift buying service during the holidays really gets hopping in the winter so all of this writing and recognition as an expert on everything sizzling hot in Minneapolis really pays off. She's conscientious about not rehashing what other local bloggers are talking about and just writes for a couple of hours a week on original subject matter. Though she says she's not a natural writer, she's trained herself to be in the habit of continual blogging because of the very engaging invitation to converse that blogging offers web surfers. Her brand is edgy, cosmopolitan, and out-of-the-box, so blogging is the perfect, ever-changing match for her.

Katharine Giovanni keeps it all together and informs her audience through her blog on www.triangleconcierge.com with travel tips and original motivational articles revolving around trust and ethics. One of her golden rules is to never post anything negative like gossip, because once it's out on the internet, it's there forever and you can't get rid of it. She's so addicted to Twitter that her husband calls her BlackBerry her "Crackberry." She adheres to agreements banning "Crackberry" use from family vacations.

Valerie Fidan says, "I do not necessarily use social media to attract new clients but it is important to have a social media presence if your audience and clients are actively on social media sites."

Brand It, Market It, and Work that Crowd!

Many business owners invest in a website that just sits there, unnoticed, because they don't understand how to use all of the wonderful web tools to illuminate their presence. With insider knowledge on how to trigger attention, you can increase your website traffic and attract new clients.

Consider the following tips from website branding, marketing guru, and author Khoa Bui.

Find Out Who Your Target Customer Is

Congratulations in taking the first step in building your first website. Now let's get to work! First, you need to know everything about your customer demographic. Make a descriptive list of your ideal client's age, gender, occupation, and interests. Remember to be as specific and narrow as possible. You'll be using this information later when writing your website copy and optimizing your website. It will also help you generate sales.

Register a Powerful Domain Name

Once you've identified your target customer, you should register your domain name. To make sure your website actually is found by potential clients, it needs to be found by the search engines first! To make sure this happens, your domain name must include the major keywords that your customer is searching with. An example of this would be www.conciergechicago.com, www.householdhelpseattle.com, and www.personalshopperminneapolis.com. Don't use your business name in your URL; remember that you want people to find you. It would be hard for the search engines to know what you do and find you if your domain was www.franklinsilverplatter.com. If you still want your business name to have its own domain, just register another domain name for it. Don't forget to include your area location as part of your domain name so people looking for your services in your area will find you, as well as a word that describes your services.

Choose a Reputable Hosting Service for Your Website

Make sure your hosting provider is fast and secure. People don't want to wait too long for your website to load and will leave your site if it's pokey. It's also important to have 24-hour tech support so you can get the help you need. Finally, make sure that your hosting provider is a reputable one and isn't prone to hacker attacks and servers crashing.

Gather Your Marketing Materials and Launch Your Website!

Collect as many testimonials, awards received, featured media works, quotes, and anything else that your business has taken part in to showcase. This will help you convert your traffic to sales. Once you've gathered all your marketing materials, you're ready to build your website, the right way! Image is everything online, so invest in a professional website design company to build your image and website for you. Never cut corners with your business.

Optimize Your Site, Increase Traffic, and Watch Your Sales Explode!

You'll start generating sales for your website by increasing its website traffic. Here are just a few ways that will help you get started:

- Write articles and submit them to ezine directories.
- Setup a new blog site and write keyword rich blog posts to attract free traffic.
- Create advertising campaigns.
- Use Facebook and Twitter.
- Create and communicate with newsletters to feature your site.
- Search engine optimize your website.
- Keep learning and applying the most current traffic generation techniques to increase your sales and sell more than ever before!

For in-depth instruction on making the web really work for you, we highly recommend Khoa's book, *How to Increase Your Website Traffic*, available at www.khoa-bui.com.

Even More Ways to Use the Internet

- Send and receive business communications to and from clients, like policies, contracts, and bills.
- Utilize online software to create and send newsletters to your clients.

- Stay tuned in to fellow concierges and vendors for helpful information exchanges through Twitter and email.
- Search review sites like www.yelp.com, www.zagat.com, www.roadfood.com, and www.urbanspoon.com for restaurant and travel dining choices for your clients.
- Order film processing, grocery orders, and schedule appointments.
- Coordinate and share scheduling and organization with your clients with online day planner tools from www.keepandshare.com.
- Use social media to create a following and expand your customer base geographically.
- Keep on top of the latest customer service methods and other topics that will give you an edge on the competition.

If you take advantage of the power of connecting to your customers as friends, the way social media allows you to do, you'll be taking part in the new way customer service is being defined. For more education on how businesses are benefiting from this new way of marketing through personal connections, read Gary Vaynerchuk's *The Thank You Economy* (HarperBusiness, 2011). The insights, tips, and suggestions in it are pure gold. You'll find it listed in the appendix.

Who's Minding the Store?
Employees and Finances

Personal concierges who decide to keep their businesses small may never need employees, while others whose businesses take off quickly find themselves working seven days a week and will need to hire some help. In this chapter, we'll take a look at some unique solutions to finding the right employees. We'll also give you tips for keeping your finances straight, and we'll talk about income statements, taxes, and other important details regarding cold, hard cash.

Help Wanted

One approach to hiring is to start off small by taking on a part-time assistant. This gives you the opportunity to assess the situation after a few months to see if you really need a full-time employee. If you aren't in the financial position to hire any help at all, perhaps you can recruit family members or friends to pitch in when necessary. Offer to buy them lunch sometime or do some errands for them in return.

New business owners can also turn to temp agencies when looking for employees. Or perhaps try to find a college student or intern. The trade-off? The student gets experience to put on her resume, and the business owner gets some much-needed help.

Growing Like a Weed

Cynthia A., the concierge from San Diego who started with a homebased business, saw her business grow so quickly that she ended up moving to an office away from home. Today, she has two partners in the business and uses the services of about 60

Tapping Into Gold

Retired professionals sometimes have too much extra time on their hands and many of them are looking for additional sources of income. Consider hiring them to answer phones, locate hard-to-find items or collectibles for clients, and run errands. It might be a good fit for both of you! Katharine Giovanni believes tapping into some of those seniors' talents and wisdom would be akin to striking gold. "I believe our retired seniors are an untapped, natural resource," she says. "Some of these people have crackerjack minds and bodies but have been forced into retirement. If they are ready to retire, fine. But if they aren't, many of these seniors would make excellent employees." Locate retired and senior workers by word of mouth, or by placing ads on www.craigslist.org, www.score.org, and www.meetup.com.

---

personal concierges who work for her as independent contractors. The independent contractors come in handy when she needs something handled in another city or state. She can simply call on her colleagues who live or work in those areas. Cynthia, who had previously worked as a hotel concierge, had all her contacts from those days and was able to use them to line up independent contractors in different cities who can work for her, as she needs them.

Several concierges we talked to use independent contractors; these concierges have larger businesses and serve some out-of-town clients. They said they usually pay an hourly rate to the independent contractors; the pay scale is agreed upon by both parties ahead of time.

"You can also hire interns and stay-at-home moms," says Katharine G. in Raleigh, North Carolina. "They have the hours available that are compatible with your needs." By the time Katharine's business was about a year old, she had two full-time employees and was expecting to hire more soon. Katharine found one of her employees by advertising her openings in local newspapers and interviewing the applicants. She said she looked for someone who was good with people, had some customer service experience, was flexible, and could handle multiple tasks.

Angela L., a personal concierge in Austin, Texas, has four full-time employees. She found two of them through word of mouth, another through a temporary agency, and the other by advertising in local newspapers. She mentioned the same type of qualifications as Katharine did, adding that she also looked for "real go-getters."

Add Seasoned Workers to Your Team

Experience Works (www.experienceworks.org) is an organization dedicated to placing seniors in the workforce. They have an admirable core belief system:

- ◯ Older people should have the opportunity to learn new skills and contribute to their communities throughout their lives.

- ◯ Employers who hire, train, and retain older workers will be most successful.

- ◯ People who are productive and active throughout their lives will have better health, increased longevity, and a positive impact on their communities.

Why not use older people for all of your employment needs? Retired baby boomers are the most educated group out there!

Angela and the other concierges who were interviewed said that, except in the case of independent contractors, their employees worked on-site and also used their own vehicles with mileage reimbursements.

Katharine G. says it is vital that your employees be bonded and have car insurance. Bonding helps ensure that your clients are protected against losses from theft or damage done by your employees, and that the bonding company will be responsible for those losses—not you. "Also, it's very important that you have contracts for each of your employees," Katharine says. "This is something we take care of immediately anytime we bring in a new employee."

While the concierges we talked to were reluctant to give specific information on the employee contracts they use, the general elements include: how many hours the employee will typically work, what kinds of duties they will perform, what the pay rate will be, whether or not they will be paid mileage, and what types of benefits they will receive.

Bright Idea

Some personal concierges with employees find it helpful to hire a payroll service that will calculate and pay employee taxes on their behalf.

Talking Insurance

If you end up hiring employees, you're required to take certain steps to help protect their health and safety. You'll need to check out the workers' compensation insurance laws in your state because the laws do vary. Workers' comp essentially covers you and

Student Aid

Want to hire a part-time employee but really don't have the funds to spare right now? You might want to look into hiring an unpaid intern. Get in touch with your local community colleges or universities and find out what requirements are in order.

Some colleges may stipulate a certain number of hours the intern must work each month, as well as what tasks they can and cannot do as part of their internship. Usually, the school will send you an application asking you to describe the job's responsibilities and your needs in terms of major, skill level, and other qualifications. Then the school will send you resumes of students who might work well with you. Each school has different requirements, so get busy and get the scoop.

your employees for any injury or illness that occurs while an employee is at work. If you have several employees, you might also want to look into offering them health benefits. There are all kinds of policies out there that provide a range of coverage including medical, dental, vision, and life insurance.

Katharine did encounter one somewhat amusing detail when it came to insurance. "The personal concierge business is so new that my insurance company didn't yet have a category for us," she says. "So I got lumped in under limousine services. It's such a brand new field that there is nowhere to go but up."

Benefits

Most of the concierges we talked to, even the ones with employees, are still fairly small operations and so don't provide full benefits to their employees even though most of them hope to be able to do so in the near future. In the meantime, some of them do try to offer bonuses when they can, along with comp time and other incentives.

As one concierge mentioned, there are some unusual fringe benefits for concierge employees, such as the occasions when a grateful client might tip really well or offer some type of small gift. Employees occasionally get to attend special events if a client has to bow out at the last minute.

Watching Your Finances

Keeping an eye on the finances is one of the most important aspects of the job for any business owner. If the cash flow isn't, well, flowing, then your business will surely suffer.

You may not be one of those people who has a way with a calculator or views bookkeeping as something fun. Let's face it, many of us just aren't gifted in the math or accounting departments. But you don't have to be a financial whiz to keep up with the basic finances of your business.

If you have the extra resources, no matter how small your business is, you can hire a bookkeeper or an accountant to keep up with that end of the business. But even if you do put those matters into someone else's hands, it's still important to be aware

> **Dollar Stretcher**
> When you're launching your business and making calls to attorneys or accountants, it doesn't hurt to ask if they have special discounts for new business owners!

of everything going on in your business. Take some time at least every few months to give the books a good once-over yourself. That's a good opportunity for you to spot any potential problems or catch anything that looks out of order.

Penny-Pinching Pointers

It's always important, especially in the early stages of a new business, to make every penny count. One way you can keep costs down is to ask for discounts from businesses you will be visiting often. For instance, if you're going to be using the same printer or courier service, let them know you'll be patronizing their place of business several times a week, if not more often. Ask them upfront about whether you can expect a discount. Don't be bashful! The worst thing that could happen is that they could say no. But more often than not, they will be glad for the repeat business and will be more than happy to offer you a discount.

Your bookkeeper or accountant can also keep you apprised of which clients are paying on time and which clients seem to have forgotten about you. If a client is notoriously late or hasn't paid you in months, you should always pay him or her a courteous visit to see if there are any complaints about the service you are providing. Remember: Customer service is an all-important part of your business, and you don't want to dismiss any clients without looking into the situation first.

Bright Idea

Why not create a separate file or folder for all documents pertaining to financial matters concerning your new business? This can include copies of contracts, insurance papers, etc. That way, those important papers will be at your fingertips when you need them. And, yes, the day will come when you will need them.

An Important Statement

You may not be familiar with an income statement, also called a profit and loss statement. It's really not that complicated, though. An income statement basically follows the collections and operating expenses of your business over a particular period of time. We've provided samples of income statements and a worksheet for you to create your own projected statements in this chapter (see pages 116 and 118, respectively).

Go ahead and spend some time on the worksheets tallying up some of your potential expenses and profits. Maybe you will find that you really have a knack for this sort of thing and will end up taking care of all of the financial details pertaining to your new business!

How Taxing

You can run, but you can't hide! No matter what type of business you own, the tax situation must be addressed. Of course, it's no fun, but it's a detail you absolutely must pay attention to. Otherwise, you could run into all kinds of tax troubles that could put a real damper on your business and even cost you money and clients. It's always better to be safe than sorry.

We've already mentioned the benefits of hiring an accountant, and that move is especially wise when it comes to your taxes. We're not going to get into lots of tax specifics here, but we do want to address the topic of deductions. When running a homebased personal concierge business, your tax deductions will be similar to just about any other homebased business. For example, you are allowed to deduct a percentage of the costs for your home office if you are using space solely as an office.

Some of the following are deductions you can claim when you have a homebased business, while others are deductions that can be taken wherever you hang your shingle. Your accountant can give you other particulars.

- *Auto expenses.* These expenses come into play any time you use your vehicle for business. For instance, when you go to the printer, post office, to visit a client, etc., keep a notebook in your vehicle so you can jot down your beginning and ending mileage. It will really come in handy when your accountant asks for your itemized expenses!
- *Phone expenses.* These include business-related phone calls and phone-service charges.
- *Entertainment expenses.* If you have a business lunch with a client, make note of it. If you present a seminar to a group of clients, you are allowed to claim the deductions for the cost of the seminar—provided the expenses were business-related.

A Receipt Receptacle

You know those snazzy recipe holders or handy coupon holders that some folks always seem to have on hand? Shop around and find one just for your business receipts. Office supply stores have that sort of thing. You could also make a homemade receipts box. Go to a craft store, get the supplies, and decorate it yourself. Maybe it will make the monotonous chore of paperwork a little more fun. OK, maybe fun isn't the right word. But you get the idea.

Income Statements

Here are monthly income statements for our two hypothetical personal concierge businesses.

Income Statements
For the month of October 20xx

	ACE	First Class
Gross Monthly Income	**$3,200**	**$9,000**
Expenses		
Rent and utilities	N/A	$1,200
Employee payroll and benefits	N/A	$1,800
Phone service	$50	$125
Internet access	$20	$50
Website maintenance	$50	$65
Advertising	$65	$100
Legal and accounting services	N/A	N/A
Insurance	$85	$165
Office supplies	$45	$125
Postage and delivery	$35	$115
Vehicle maintenance and mileage	$100	$175
Subscriptions and dues	$25	$50
Miscellaneous	$55	$120
Total Monthly Expenses	**$530**	**$4,090**
Net Monthly Profit	**$2,670**	**$4,910**

- *Business supplies and equipment expenses*, as long as they are used solely for business. It's very important that you keep a log of which items were used for business and which items, if any, were for personal use. Your accountant—and more importantly, the IRS—may raise the question at a later date, and you'll want to have the answer ready.

Smart Tip

Don't forget to keep your receipts and other records separate from your personal finances if you are functioning as a sole proprietor.

- *Business-related travel expenses*. No, you can't deduct that trip to visit your sister who just had a baby. Sorry, you can't deduct that weekend getaway, either. Any travel deductions must be for business-related purposes, such as a seminar or some other event pertaining to your business.
- *Meals and hotel expenses*. The above advice also goes for this category. You are allowed to claim the deductions if attending a seminar, convention, or other business-related event. Unsure if you can claim a particular meal or hotel deduction? Ask your accountant!

It's also important to remember that concierges should never take deductions for expenses reimbursed by clients. Taxes are a special concern for those who have employees because there are all sorts of rules dictated by the IRS and state tax boards for employers. For personal concierges who provide only basic types of services, there should be few special tax issues. If in doubt, consult your attorney or tax expert.

You might also want an attorney to take a look at any contracts you sign with clients or employees and provide advice on other business matters as well. Early on, it's wise to establish a rapport with someone who has the expertise you will need at some point down the road.

Income Statement Worksheet

For the month of _____

Gross Monthly Income	$
Expenses	
Rent and utilities	$
Employee payroll and benefits	
Phone service	
Internet access	
Website maintenance	
Advertising	
Legal and accounting services	
Insurance	
Office supplies	
Postage and delivery	
Vehicle maintenance and mileage	
Subscriptions and dues	
Miscellaneous	
Total Monthly Expenses	$
Net Monthly Profit	$

It's a Pleasure

All the personal concierges interviewed for this book agreed on one thing—now is the time to jump in! The field is wide open, and there's a need for professional, hard-working, customer service-oriented personal concierges. The demand is increasing, and someone will need to supply the service. It might as well be you!

Top Ten Secrets of Success

Any good personal concierge should possess certain qualities. Here are a few of those keys to success:

1. Be flexible.
2. Have an abundance of patience.
3. Be resourceful.
4. Be well-organized.
5. Provide excellent customer service.
6. Be a good time manager.
7. Be a self-starter.
8. Be willing to network.
9. Be ready to juggle multiple projects.
10. Be honest, trustworthy, and dependable.

By reading this business guide, you've already taken the first step on the road to success. As you continue down that road, keep in mind that the definition of success varies from one personal concierge to another. For instance, a busy stay-at-home mother may consider her personal concierge business a success because working with a handful of flexible clients gives her some additional income while allowing her to be at home when she needs to be. Another concierge who caters to corporate clients may feel that success means being able to juggle 20 demanding, well-paying clients at all hours of the day or night. As with most things in life, success is in the eye of the beholder.

Any Regrets?

Most of the concierges interviewed had very few regrets about how they launched their businesses, but some would make changes if they could go back and start over. "I wish I had started it a lot sooner," says Katharine G., the concierge from Raleigh, North Carolina. "I realize now how big a demand there is going to be for these types of services."

Many of the concierges we spoke to also had a few words of advice for people considering getting into the business. Make sure you have enough money saved up to go out on your own. Larissa E. laments, "If I could change anything, I would have continued working to save enough money to last me a year instead of six months. I didn't believe what everyone else told me (or what I read in black and white) when everyone said it would take a solid year and sometimes two years to really get the business going." Abbie M. cautions, "Clients don't arrive overnight. You need to educate them first and then get them started. I think a lot of people believe that because this is such a great business idea that everyone else will realize it too and just come on board."

Kellye G. recommends, "Find your particular niche. It's hard to be everything to everyone." And Loreine G. reminds us, "If you do not genuinely like people and want them to succeed, this is not the industry for you. Remain open minded, flexible, and truly care about your clients." And Jennifer C. goes for the practical advice, "Make sure you have insurance from day one." Three concierges we interviewed wished they had a partner with complimentary and opposite skills from the beginning so that they could have focused just on the areas they were good at. It's hard to find the right person, though and two are still open to it and looking for the right fit through close referrals.

Valerie Fidan gives advice to help newbies avoid frustration, "I've learned over time that it is alright to decline a client. As a newbie, you want to take on each and every client prospect but you have to learn to say no. This is the amazing part about running your own business, you are the deciding factor if a client prospect is a great fit with your company culture, the way your company operates and of course personalities.

> **Tip...**
>
> **Smart Tip**
>
> You'll probably get phone calls from people who will ask you to explain what a concierge is or to describe exactly what you do. Write a short description of your business (like your elevator speech) and keep it handy so you can launch right into a quick explanation when you get one of those calls while you're trying to juggle five other things.

"Over the course of the years I've learned how to deal with and manage certain personalities. When conducting client consults, this is the perfect opportunity for me to pick up on certain traits by asking numerous questions regarding their project, work style, preferences, and tastes. If I ever feel someone does not fit our work style, I decline to pursue a working relationship and refer him to a different concierge with a better matching company culture and work style."

You're on Your Way

The fact that you've reached the end of this book is cause for celebration because it means you're serious about your new business. So serious that you've read an entire book about it, studied worksheets, listened to the opinions of other personal concierges, and soaked up tips and advice from some experts.

You've come a long way, baby. But you still have a long way to go because now you need to begin the work required to make your business a reality—and a success. People all over your city need personal concierges. They need you. So what are you waiting for? Go make a name for yourself!

Appendix
Personal Concierge Resources

It's pretty obvious after studying how a concierge works that creating a continual flow of resources to dip into is essential if you want to be incredible at it. Resources lead to other resources if you discipline yourself to habitually expose yourself to new leads, dig deep into interesting arts and entertainment news, and always ask for new connections. There is no end of the line as far as resources go and understanding that your own creativity in multiplying them is essential in determining your success.

From picking the brains of other sassy entrepreneurs to reading what's hot off the press in the world of innovative entrepreneurship, these networking methods can lead to a powerful education that can't be purchased. All of this resource digging and education is part of networking. Therefore, we present you with a wealth of sources to check into, check out, and harness for your own personal information multiplication blitz.

These sources are tidbits, ideas to get you started on your own research. They are by no means the only sources out there and should not be taken as the ultimate answer. We have done our research, but businesses tend to move, change, fold, and expand rapidly. As we have repeatedly stressed, do your homework. Get out and start investigating.

Associations

International Concierge and Lifestyle Management Association (ICLMA), 3650 Rogers Road, #328, Wake Forest, NC 27587, (800) 376-7020, www.iclma.org

National Association of Professional Organizers (NAPO), 15000 Commerce Parkway, Suite C, Mount Laurel, NJ 08054, (856) 380-6828, Fax: (856) 439-0525, www. napo.net

National Concierge Association, 2920 Idaho Avenue North, Minneapolis, MN 55427, (612) 253-5110, fax: (612) 317-2910, www.nationalconciergeassociation.com

Washington Area Concierge Association, 1200 Pennsylvania Ave., N.W., P.O. Box 167, Washington, DC 20004, www.wacaonline.com

The Concierge manual
+ Going Above & Beyond by Katharine C. Giovanni

Books, Booklets, and Magazines

Built to Serve—How to Drive the Bottom Line with People First Practices, Dan J. Sanders, United Supermarkets Ltd., McGraw-Hill

Celeb Staff Magazine, Golden Eagle Publishing House Inc., 9201 Wilshire Blvd., Suite 205, Beverly Hills, CA 90210, (310) 273-9176, www.celebstaff.com, subscriptions@ celebstaff.com

Confessions of a Concierge: Madame Lucie's History of Twentieth-Century France, Bonnie G. Smith, Yale University Press, http://yalepress.yale.edu

Engage!—The Complete Guide for Brands and Businesses to Cultivate and Measure Success in the New Web, Brian Solis, John Wiley and Sons Inc.

Delivering Happiness—A Path to Profits Passion and Purpose, Tony Hsieh, Business Plus, Hachette Book Group, www.hachettebookgroup.com

Entrepreneur Magazine, Entrepreneur Media Inc., (800) 274-6229, www.entrepreneur. com

Facebook Marketing—Leverage Social Media to Grow Your Business, Steven Holzner, Que Publishing

Green Lodging News, Hasek Communications LLC, www.greenlodgingnews.com

How to Increase Your Website Traffic, Khoa Bui, Entrepreneur Press

How to Make Money with YouTube, Brad and Debra Schepp, McGraw-Hill

The Celebrity Assistant's Handbook: How To Successfully Work with Celebrities, Billionaires, and The Top One Percent, C.S. Copeland, www.personalassistantguide. com

Inc. Magazine, Mansueto Ventures LLC, (800) 234-0999, www.inc.com

The Concierge: Key to Hospitality, McDowell Bryson and Adele Ziminski, John Wiley & Sons, www.wiley.com

How to Start and Operate an Errand Service, Rob Spina, Legacy Marketing

The Concierge Manual: A Step-by-Step Guide to Starting Your Own Concierge Service or Lifestyle Management Company, 3rd Ed., Katharine C. Giovanni and Ron Giovanni, NewRoad Publishing, www.katharinegiovanni.com

Think and Grow Rich, Napoleon Hill, Tribeca Books

The Everything Guide to Social Media, John K. Waters, Adams Media, www. everything.com

The Thank You Economy, Gary Vaynerchuk, HarperCollins Publishers

The Tipping Point: How Little Things Can Make a Big Difference, Malcolm Gladwell, Backbay Books

12 Steps to a Worry-Free Retirement, Daniel Kehrer, Kiplinger Washington Editors Inc., Random House

Who, Geoff Smart and Randy Street, ghSMART and Company Inc., Random House

Zingerman's Guide to Giving Great Service, Ari Weinzweig, Hyperion

Concierge Consultants

Triangle Concierge, Katharine Giovanni, 3650 Rogers Road, # 328, Wake Forest, NC 27587, (888) 418-1999, www.triangleconcierge.com, kgiovanni@triangleconcierge. com

Concierge At Large, Inc., PO Box 2628, La Mesa, CA 91941-2628, www.concierge-at-large.com, info@conciergeatlarge.com

Concierge Networks

Concierge Association of the Palm Beaches, www.conciergeassociationpb.org

▲

Concierge Network on LinkedIn, www.linkedin.com/groups/Concierge-Network-60692

CORE System, Concierge At Large Network Inc., PO Box 2628, La Mesa, CA 91941-2628, No telephone inquiries please. Submit inquiry via email to info@ conciergeatlarge.com

Greater Boston Concierge Association, 304 Newbury Street, #526, Boston, MA 02115, www.gbcaonline.com, gbca@hotmail.com

St. Louis Concierge Service Association, PO Box 515103, Saint Louis, MO 63151, (314) 747-3335, www.stlconcierge.org

The Butler Bureau, www.thebutlerbureau.com

Personal Assistant Pro, (901) 850-9030, www.personalassistantpro.com

Education, Training, Conferences, and Events

Annual Hospitality Industry Symposium, University of San Francisco School of Business and Professional Studies, 2130 Fulton Street, San Francisco, CA, 94117-1080, (415) 422-5555, www.usfca.edu/bps/hospitality/The_Annual_Hospitality_Industry_Symposium/

Starkey International Institute for Household Management, 1350 Logan Street, Denver, Colorado 80203, (800) 888-4904, www.starkeyintl.com

Leadership Summit, National Concierge Association, 2920 Idaho Avenue North, Minneapolis, MN 55427, (612) 253-5110, fax: (612) 317-2910, www.national conciergeassociation.com

The Concierge Master's Seminar, Triangle Concierge, 3650 Rogers Road, #328, Wake Forest, NC 27587, (888) 418-1999, www.triangleconcierge.com, kgiovanni@ triangleconcierge.com

Certified Concierge Specialist Program (CCS) and Annual Conference, International Concierge and Lifestyle Management Association (ICLMA), 3650 Rogers Road, #328, Wake Forest, NC 27587, (800) 376-7020, www.iclma.org

Basic and Advanced Concierge Training, Concierge Resource, 700 Kalamath Street, Denver, CO 80204, (303) 883-8001, www.conciergeresource.com

GBCA Annual Trade Show, www.gbcaonline.com/events.html, joed@artsboston.org

NAPO Annual Conference and Organizing Exposition, San Diego, CA, (856) 380-6828, www.cgallagher@ahint.com, napo.net/conference

NEWH Leadership Conference, Orlando, FL, www.newh.org/leadership-conference/leadership-conference, jena.seibel@newh.org

NEWH, Inc. The Hospitality Industry Network, PO Box 322, Shawano, WI 54166, (800) 593-6394, fax: (800) 693-6394, www.newh.org

Employment

The CPAI Group Inc., (Celebrity Personal Assistants), 3475 Lenox Road, Suite 400, Atlanta, GA 30326, (866) 867-7672, www.celebritypersonalassistants.com, info@celebritypersonalassistants.com

The Celebrity Personal Assistant Network, Brian Daniel, 14510 Big Basin Way, Suite 191, Saratoga, CA 95070, (310) 866-7128, www.FindCelebrityJobs.com, CelebAssistant@live.com

The Help Company, Los Angeles, San Francisco, and New York, (888) HELP-880, www.thehelpcompany.com, claudia@thehelpcompany.com

Cruise Ship Jobs, www.cruiseshipjobs77.com

Newsletters

CONDÉ NAST, www.Concierge.com, concierge.com/services/newsletter

NAPO News, National Association of Professional Organizers, 4700 W. Lake Ave, Glenview, IL 60025, (847) 375-4746, fax: (877) 734-8668, www.napo.net

Personal Assistant Pro, (901) 850-9030, ext. 114, www.personalassistantpro.com

Quintessentially, 353 Lexington Avenue, 3rd Floor, New York, NY 10016, (800) 444-7846, www.quintessentially.com/newsletters/2011-04-26/, membershipusa@quintessentially.com

Online Forums

iVillage.com's Message Forums, go to www.forums.ivillage.com, then type "concierge" in the All iVillage search box.

Yahoo Concierge Groups, go to www.finance.dir.groups.yahoo.com, then type "concierge" in the search box for group listings.

Software

Clickfree Automatic Backup Software, by Storage Appliance Corporation, (866) 680-0516, www.clickfree.com

eCRM3 (Electronic Concierge Resource Management Software), Concierge Resource, 700 Kalamath Street, Denver, CO 80204, (303) 883-8001, www.conciergeresource.com

The Concierge Assistant, Gold Key Solutions, 28118 Agoura Road, Suite 202, Agoura Hills, CA 91301, (818) 865-0006, fax: (818) 597-2389, www.goldkeysolutions.com, info@GoldKeySolutions.com

Virtual Assistant Manager, StormSource Software Inc., 109 Stevenson Street, Suite 200, San Francisco, California 94105, (480) 483-1199, www.virtualassistantmanager.com, sales@virtualassistantmanager.com

Sage ACT! 2011, (866) 873-2006, www.act.com

Social Media Gurus

Chris Brogan, www.chrisbrogan.com

Gary Vaynerchuk, www.garyvaynerchuk.com, vaynermedia.com, 220 E. 23rd Street, Suite 605, New York, NY, 10010, info@vaynermedia.com

Guy Kawasaki, www.guykawasaki.com, kawasaki@garage.com

Khoa Bui, Khoa Bui International, 243/1 Heritage Cove, Maylands 6051, Western Australia, (08) 6102 1277, www.khoa-bui.com, support@khoa-bui.com

Shannon Paul, (734) 968-9065, www.veryofficialblog.com, shannonpaul5@gmail.com

Successful General Concierge Services

Chicago's Girl on the Go, Chicago, IL, (312) 371-0596, www.chicagosgirlonthego.com

Cowtown Concierge Services, 3424 Pelham, Ft. Worth, TX 76116, (817) 737-2665, www.cowtownconcierge.com, kellye@cowtownconcierge.com

Concierge by the Sea, PO Box 740, Lewes, DE 19958, (877) 302.BEACH, www.conciergebythesea.com, customerservice@conciergebythesea.com

In a New York Minute Concierge Service, LLC, PO Box 131, LaGrangeville, NY 12540, www.inanyminute.net, (845) 797-4314, thesimplelife@inanyminute.net

Jennifer Cochran, Warp Speed Errands, PO Box 6587, Gainesville, GA 30504, (770) 654-WARP, www.warpspeederrands.com, info@warpspeederrands.com

Jennifer Knoch, Radar Concierge, Minneapolis, MN, (612) 532-3789, www.radar-msp.com, jen@radar-msp.com

Lifestyle Elements, P.O. Box 570, Torrensville Adelaide, South Australia, 5031, Australia, +61 (08) 8292 2286, fax: +61 (08) 8311 5288, www.lifestyleelements.com.au, info@lifestyleelements.com.au

Lindsey Doolittle, At Your Service Event Planning and Promotional Items, Minneapolis, MN, (651) 332-1061, www.lindseysevents.com, info@lindseysevents.com

Ms. Errands, Springfield, MO, (417) 224-2050, fax: (417) 224-2050, www.mserrands.com, larissa@mserrands.com

Purveyors of Time, 815 Moraga Drive, Suite 310, Los Angeles, CA 90049, (310) 471-7151, www.purveyorsoftimecom, info@purveyorsoftime.com

Triangle Concierge Inc., 3650 Rogers Road, #328, Wake Forest, NC 27587, (888) 418-1999, www.triangleconcierge.com, kgiovanni@triangleconcierge.com

Warp Speed Errands, PO Box 6587, Gainesville, GA 30504, (770) 654-WARP (9277), www.warpspeederrands.com, blog: errandgoddess.wordpress.com, info@warpspeederrands.com

Shopgirl, Park City, UT (435) 513-0242, www.shopgirlparkcity.com, fonda@shopgirlparkcity.com

Silvia Oppenheim, Le Concierge SF, San Francisco, CA, (415) 602-6652, www.leconciergesf.com, silvia@leconciergesf.com

Wise Women, Oklahoma City, OK, (405) 360-7474, www.wisewomen4hire.com, info@wisewomen4hire.com

Successful Niche Concierge Services

Archibald Relocation, 6650 SW Redwood Lane, Suite 220, Portland, OR 97224, (877) 726-7724, www.archibaldrelocation.com, info@archibladrelocation.com

Best Upon Request Corporate Inc., 8170 Corporate Park Drive, Suite 300, Cincinnati, OH 45242, (513) 605-7800, www.bestuponrequest.com, info@bestuponrequest.com

Complete Concierge, Marina Del Rey, CA, (310) 466-1062, www.completeconcierge.com, info@completeconcierge.com

Distinctive Lifestyle, 1815 Griffin Road, Suite 404, Dania Beach, FL 33004, (954) 926-2940, fax: (954) 920-5312, www.dstyle.com, info@dstyle.com

Elder Concierge Services, 1807 South Pearl Street, Denver, CO 80210, (720) 217-8137, www.elderconciergeservices.com, info@elderconciergeservices.com

Brian Mahan, Enlightened Concierge, Beverly Hills, CA, (310) 991-3231, www.enlightenedconcierge.com, brian@enlightenedconcierge.com

Escort Assistant, www.escortassistant.net, assistant@escortassistant.net

Hey Cosmo, Arsenal Interactive Inc., 2672 Bayshore Parkway, Suite 808, Mountain View, CA 94043, (650) 282-2900, www.heycosmo.com, support@heycosmo.com

The Grocery Girls, Park City, UT, (866) 278-2254, orders@thegrocerygirls.com, www.thegrocerygirls.com

Kevin Miller, The Daily Plan It Inc., 1106 NE 16th Court #1, Fort Lauderdale, FL 33305, (954) 732-9066, www.thedailyplanit.info, yourdailyplanit@yahoo.com

Mumcierge, Dubai, UAE, (+97) 150 6408322, www.mumcierge.com, info@mumcierge.ae

Privé International, (888) 834-9997 www.priveinternational.com info@priveinternational.com

Valerie Fidan, Valerie A. Lifestyle Management, 26 Arroyo View Circle, Belmont, CA 94002, (650) 394-5090, www.valeriea.com, info@valeria.com

Miscellaneous Service and Vendor Connections

ElJet Aviation Services, U.S. Private Jet Charter Flights, 110 South Fairfax, Suite A11-129, Los Angeles, CA 90036, (888) 355-3538, www.ellejet.com

Glossary

Alternative office: office space that deviates from the norm, such as space shared with another professional or noncompeting business.

Concierge: someone in the business of fulfilling the requests of guests or clients; term evolved from the French *comte des cierges*, the keeper of the candles, who attended to the whims of visiting noblemen at medieval castles; today there are hotel concierges, corporate concierges, and personal concierges.

Corporate concierge: an employee hired by a corporation to serve the firm's other employees by running errands, picking up dry-cleaning, ordering dinner, etc.

Domain name: a website or internet address. Sometimes referred to as a URL (Uniform Resource Location).

DSL: short for Digital Subscriber Line, it's a high speed internet connection that is always on. Typical connections allow users to receive data at 1.5 Mbps and send data at approximately 256 Kbps, rather than the 56Kbps of a standard dial-up connection. In most cases, you can keep a single line for both phone and DSL connections.

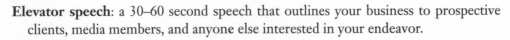

Elevator speech: a 30–60 second speech that outlines your business to prospective clients, media members, and anyone else interested in your endeavor.

Employee Dishonesty Bonds: a bond to protect a business owner from employees acting dishonestly during the course of their job.

Feng shui: the Chinese art of promoting a more harmonious flow of energy, or chi, in one's home or office.

Gold keys: the emblem adopted by the organization Les Clefs d'Or; a hotel concierge wearing crossed gold keys on his or her lapel is a member of Les Clefs d'Or.

Hotel concierge: an employee hired by a hotel to assist guests with needs that arise during their stay, such as making dinner reservations, arranging tours, and offering advice on shopping or sightseeing.

Les Clefs d'Or: a French term that means keys of gold; a 70-year-old professional organization of the top hotel concierges in the world. The website for the USA organization (with more than 450 members in over 30 states) is http://www.lcdusa.org/.

Limited Liability Company: known commonly as LLC, the term describes a way to structure your business that allows you to run your business while keeping your personal assets separate. Unlike sole proprietors, owners of LLCs can normally keep their house, investments, and other personal property even if their business fails.

Membership fees: charges collected by some concierges that allow clients a certain number of requests each month.

Mission statement: a statement that defines a company's goals and how it expects to achieve them.

Perks: the extras—such as concierge services, hair salons, espresso bars, and film processing—that some corporations provide for their employees.

Personal concierge: not employed by a hotel or corporation; instead, markets services directly to clients who pay for errand running, gift buying, making travel arrangements, etc.

Referral fees: payments from various companies given to concierges for directing business their way.

S-Corporation: a method to set up a small business (less than 100 shareholders) and avoid paying double taxes.

Sole Proprietorship: a business structure under which the business owner can be held personally liable for any business-related obligation.

Vendors: businesses used by concierges to provide their clients with various services, such as florists, caterers, and wedding planners.

Index